Nos
Vo

MUNICIPAL REFUSE COLLECTION VEHICLES

Barrie C Woods

Trans-Pennine Publishing

CONTENTS

Front Cover:
In the 1920s and '30s, this is the type of refuse vehicle that would visit your street on a regular basis. Still going strong after 70 years, this beautifully restored Shelvoke & Drewry Freighter was in service with Epsom & Ewell UDC. The red and white scarf hanging from the side of the cab is the equivalent of our flashing amber beacon.

Rear Cover Top:
This old S&D side loader (purchased by the Borough of Ealing in the 1940s) has reached the end of the road and in 1998 it is seen rusting in a scrap yard just 3 miles from where it was built.

Rear Cover Bottom:
Another S&D product, this time a 1970 model TBN equipped with a fore & aft body and sealed rear door for use on night soil collections. After doing 71,855 miles by 1982 it was retired and later superbly restored by its owners Sheffield City Council. Sheffield City Council

Title Page:
A line-up of Bedford TJ chassis with Eagle bodies; these bodies (probably for export) were loaded at the side and the refuse was crushed to the rear by an ejection wall system, which also assisted in discharge. Vauxhall Motors Ltd

This Page:
A 1950s scene on a Sheffield street, with a Shefflex dustless loader discharging bins into the body by a wire pulley system. Sheffield City Council

Right:
Although a popular commercial chassis, this Bedford O type at Chatham was not common on refuse collection vehicles. The side loading body, on the other hand, was quite typical in Britain during the 1940s and '50s. Vauxhall Motors Ltd.

The **Nostalgia Road** Series ™
is conceived, designed and published
by

Trans-Pennine Publishing Ltd.
PO Box 10
Appleby-in-Westmorland
Cumbria, CA16 6FA
Tel. 017683 51053 Fax. 017683 53558
e-mail trans.pennine@virgin.net
(A Quality Guild registered company)

Reprographics
Barnabus Design & Repro
Threemilestone, Truro
Cornwall, TR4 9AN
01872 241185

And Printed in Cumbria by
Kent Valley Colour Printers Ltd.
Shap Road Industrial Estate
Kendal, Cumbria LA9 6NZ
01539 741344

© Trans-Pennine Publishing & B. C. Woods 1999
Photographs: As credited, otherwise author's collection

INTRODUCTION

When asked to research this project I had the sudden realisation that although I had worked in the refuse collection vehicle industry for some 20 years I had little knowledge of its origins. Obviously I knew of the earlier types of lorries, systems of collection and the involvement of local authorities, but the how, why and where of it all was another matter altogether! Indeed, I soon realised that to tell the history of refuse collection vehicles, I also needed to tell a much wider story, for a description of the vehicles without an explanation of their work would make no sense at all. Furthermore, the construction, development and operation of these vehicles is so specialised, that it required an approach that would take the reader back to the very earliest of days of refuse collection. Accordingly my research work has been most invigorating and educational, which in turn are the precise qualities that I hope I will bring to this book.

At the outset may I say that I am most grateful for the invaluable assistance of the Institute of Wastes Management, for without their generous assistance this book would simply not have been possible! In addition many refuse vehicle manufacturers, and local authorities have provided further useful information and photos.

I must record a special debt of gratitude to both Vauxhall Motors and Sheffield City Council, on whose photographs I have drawn heavily. The wonderful selection of images that these, and others, have made available for this book really do illustrate the topic well and rarely have they been seen in a general publication before. As a result they make a fascinating source of reference, especially if one moves rapidly to compare the early vehicles with the more recent ones. By this action one can fully appreciate the amazing advances in mechanisation that have transpired over the period covered. Furthermore, this is a factor that has proceeded apace to date.

As you will appreciate, the refuse industry is all about throwing things away, and I suppose my qualifications for joining the industry stem from when I 'threw away' the benefits of a Grammar School education to become a chef of all things! However, after six years of that and an increasing yearning to drive lorries, I decided to 'throw away' that career as well. I duly found a position at the famous Shelvoke & Drewry in Letchworth as a demonstration driver. Shelvoke & Drewry, or S&D as they were colloquially known had been at the forefront of the refuse collection vehicle business almost since mechanical vehicles came into being.

It was a good opportunity for me to take a position that entailed driving one of their own fleet of demonstrator vehicles (they had about a dozen at the time) around local authorities for evaluation and testing. For a week at a time we would take the vehicle (we never called them dustcarts) to some town or other, where it would be driven around the area on the normal rounds complete with the local crew picking up refuse (we never call it rubbish). This enabled the local council to compare our latest offering with both their existing machines and those of our competitors.

After some three years of this I decided to try to progress on to sales, when the opportunity came up at another RCV manufacturer in Letchworth, Arenco-Alite. This was a division of the Swedish Match Company that built the Norba refuse collection vehicle, but the firm also built many other things including toothpaste tube filling machines and fish gutting equipment! I stayed with Arenco for 16 years through various take-overs and mergers. The Company became Norba UK, and subsequently Multilift Ltd. (a division of Partek, a massive Finnish Company that built Roll-on/Roll-off equipment amongst other things).

After some time in the sales office I graduated to outside sales on all product lines, and then on to two new ranges of equipment, tipping gears and tail-lifts, before eventually becoming Marketing & Exports Manager. I left in 1988 to run my own restaurant, which I did successfully for 8 years prior to my current semi-retirement! In 1996 a casual conversation with Alan Earnshaw led to my interest in the history of refuse collection vehicles being awakened, and three years on from this I am pleased to offer this book on a subject that has never before been covered in transport publishing.

The topic is an unusual one, and it is perhaps not to everyone's taste. However, it is an absorbing subject and covers a range of everyday vehicles that greatly benefit all our lives. My return to the industry to research this book was a welcome one, and many of my old colleagues and contemporaries have greatly assisted my work. In more ways than one it has been a real trip down Nostalgia Road, I hope you enjoy the journey as much as I have!

Barrie Woods,
Letchworth, July 1999

The problem of refuse disposal has always been most acute in big cities, and London is a classic example. In this picture we see how Lambeth Borough Council refuse vehicles (Commers) are tipping locally collected refuse in a yard alongside the River Thames whilst AEC bulk carriers wait to take it out of the city - see page 27.

IN THE BEGINNING

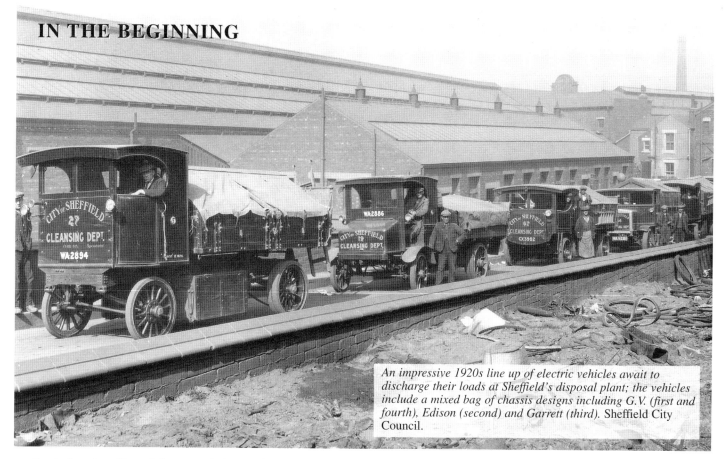

An impressive 1920s line up of electric vehicles await to discharge their loads at Sheffield's disposal plant; the vehicles include a mixed bag of chassis designs including G.V. (first and fourth), Edison (second) and Garrett (third). Sheffield City Council.

Surely the adage 'from little acorns do large oaks grow' was never more appropriate than when applied to refuse collection. From the day Eve gave Adam the apple (and he threw away the core) refuse collection has grown to a multi-million pound industry that is spread throughout the world today. In fact ever since Adam and Eve, mankind has been producing rubbish. As their descendants began to colonise the earth their intelligence brought forth a life style different from all other species, and this lifestyle produced debris that could not be used or re-cycled in some way.

The problem of disposing of this rubbish was compounded when man found that by staying put he could survive much better. He could produce food by farming, and he could build shelter to live in to protect him from the weather and wild animals. A good location may produce an abundance of animals to hunt, from which food, tools and clothing could be obtained. So instead of eating and moving on, and in consequence leaving behind his rubbish, man stockpiled his debris near to where he lived.

Doubtless after a short while any rubbish, particularly the natural type, would begin to smell! Apart from seeds, fruit husks and skins, there would be animal remains and of course human waste. Inevitably the smells emanating from the stockpiles would become intolerable, especially on a hot day! So even our ancient man found that he had two choices, either to move on, or to move the rubbish.

As the latter was obviously the simpler solution, the first refuse collections began, albeit this first move would probably be better described as 'disposal'. Archaeologists have discovered that pits or holes would be found, or dug with crude tools, and the refuse would be pushed into them. Covering the holes when they became full would be found to be further improvement, and as early as 4,000 years BC 'landfill' was in progress. What is more, its a system that is still in use today! Funnily enough, I am reliably informed that these refuse dumps have since proved to be a great source of historical information, and the archaeologists get very excited on finding them and digging them up with tiny trowels - strange chaps!

Above: *Refuse has always been associated with smells, and this vehicle is a prime example as it was Sheffield City's fish collection unit. The body is mounted on a Dennis Heron chassis with a 7' 6" wheelbase. The pungent smell associated with rotting fish must have made this one of the least pleasant jobs in refuse collection, but fish markets all over Britain required regular collection services, and many authorities developed special services for this type of waste. A large number made the process self-financing, and the waste was sold for either pet-food production or for use in fertilisers.* Sheffield City Council.

Refuse was originally a natural by-product of the cycle of life whether it was from plants, animals, birds or sea creatures. Inevitably it became part of the food chain; it produced further life or sustained that existing. It rotted naturally and kept apace with all other of nature's activities, and therefore was largely recyclable. As soon as man began to settle he upset that natural cycle so he was forced to take steps to counteract the imbalance. The landfill system that began five or six thousand years ago is still by far the most common form of disposal. However to maximise its potential many 'western' countries pre-treat the refuse by incineration, compaction, composting or by the recycling of useful materials, thus reducing the quantity prior to final disposal.

Throughout the world in general the 'Rubbish Tip' is still an every-day sight and smell! As man became more 'domesticated' and homes were built of more substantial materials, he began to produce 'artificial' products from more durable natural resources, such as bricks, cement, iron or fabrics, which in turn (when finished with) would not rot down in the normal time span. This is true of many other materials he uses, and even today biodegradable production is still in its infancy.

As a result additional refuse was produced over and above the natural wastage and, accordingly, as this refuse collected it took therefore took longer to decompose or break down due to man's interference.

The human being is basically lazy and for centuries the tendency was to throw the refuse out into the back yard or more likely into the street. In rural areas, where space was not such a premium the trend was to bury it. In the growing towns and cities, especially after the industrial revolution, 'middens' or 'netty's' became commonplace in the back of homes where all waste was thrown. The 'fines' (ashes and the like) were ousted with vegetable matter, animal bones, meat, crockery, glass and human waste. As the pile and inevitable stench grew, something needed to be resolved and communal 'middens' or 'midden heaps' appeared in convenient locations.

This obviously didn't solve the increasing problem, indeed if anything it heightened it. The proximity of refuse to human habitation inevitably brought with it disease culminating in the two major epidemics of Bubonic Plague in the 14th and 16th centuries, which was spread by flea-infested rats that fed on the refuse. Millions of people were affected, and roughly one-third of the world's population died. In its wake, the alchemists and physicians of the day began to call for ways of improving sanitation.

Sanitation was certainly needed for the situation was dire, and the streets were literally awash with human waste and rubbish. Drastic action was called for, but it was a long time coming! Some management of refuse had begun, but due to the nature of the job no one wanted to do the disposal work. Improvement Acts were passed in the 18th-century empowering Parishes, Burgomasters and Police Commissioners to clean up the streets. In 1792 the Police Commissioners were empowered to provide a twice-weekly cart to all homes. A bell would be rung to herald the approach of the vehicle, the collection became known as the 'Bell-Ash Collection'.

This was the first organised attempt at re-locating refuse to more acceptable sites. Again moving rotting waste was a most disgusting job, shovelling it up into a horse-drawn cart often from a hole in the garden, or from the communal site where it had been quietly brewing for weeks or months at a time. Doubtless there was a long queue for that job!

The hole in the garden eventually became the well-known and still commonly used 'cesspit'. The extent of the problem that this caused may be difficult to imagine, but it may be appreciated when we reveal that the City of Manchester had over 60,000 open cesspits at the time. These pits often overflowed and whilst some of the effluent got into the few sewers then existing, much of it flowed into open watercourses causing contamination of drinking water. In some locations it was recorded that up to 12 households had to share just one convenience, so it is easy to appreciate just how quickly the cesspits were filled up! Around the same time it was calculated that Glasgow had over 30,000 tons of refuse stockpiled at various sites inside the city itself! Again it defies imagination just what it was like to live near these locations on a hot summer's day!

THE LAW COMES IN

The Municipal Corporations Act of 1835 initiated our current laws covering the collection and disposal of refuse. Prior to this Municipal Corporations (such as they were) had been created by the Crown and Royal Charter and were administered by local Aldermen or Burgesses. Local governments, which had been set up by Parliament in the 19th-century, were empowered to act upon the aforementioned problems and organise the disposal of all solid and liquid waste. Landfill sites were established outside the towns and villages, often using the very locations where digging or quarrying had taken place in order to provide the construction materials for the buildings in the community.

As the communities developed, toilet facilities for the new houses were first proposed and then insisted on. These earth or ash closets were usually built in small sheds or huts outside in the garden of dwellings where possible, and were followed by the now famous 'ELSAN' chemical toilet. In 1846 the Baths and Wash-houses Act permitted local authorities to erect bath-houses where, for various reasons of cost or space, such as in areas of terraced houses or tenement blocks, homes couldn't provide any washing provision.

Above: *An obviously new electric Garrett supplied to the Borough of Hampstead in the early 1920s. Showing no awareness of the operational dangers, the loader climbs up a ladder with a heavy bin, but it takes little imagination to realise how precarious this job would be on a wet day.* Suffolk Record Office

In 1848 the Public Health Act set up a General Board of Health in London, and this was quickly followed around the country as local Boards of Health were instituted where 10% of the populace demanded it. In places where the death rate attributable to poor living conditions was in excess of 23 per 1,000, provision of such a Board became a statutory obligation. In 1866 the Sanitary Act provided another step forward, when local authorities were forced to provide adequate water, waste and sewage disposal. Systems of sewerage pipes were dug to feed sewage and waste water from houses to points where it could discharge into either rivers or the sea depending on the location of the town. Many of these Victorian sewers are still in use today! The year 1871 saw the creation of the Local Government Board, to supervise the work of local councils and take over the general responsibilities of public health.

Above: *At this point in time it might seem difficult to appreciate that this would once have been the scene in a typical council yard at the end of a day's work. The carts are all empty and the last horse is about to be unhitched after a day tramping around the streets of Manchester.* Bob Whewell

Below: *This Alex Laurie trailer, supplied to the Royal Burgh of Inverness, shows a novel way of overcoming the common problem of high loading heights that were associated with horse-drawn trailers. This vehicle features a swan-neck built in to the frame which allowed the body to be located much lower. It also features rear brakes, pneumatic tyres and hand-operated tipping gear, which were quite advanced for their day.* Robert Grieves

ALEX. LAURIE & SONS
TRAILER & MOTOR BODY BUILDERS
FALKIRK

The 1875 Public Health Act was introduced under the auspices of Prime Minister Disraeli, and it is this Act that forms the basis of our current legislation for Health & Hygiene today. The Act encompassed and consolidated the many earlier Acts throughout the country with the exception of London and Scotland which both had their own separate Acts. This major piece of legislation empowered local authorities to remove household refuse, cleanse earth closets, middens, ashpits, privies and cesspits as well as cleaning the streets. Various amendments were introduced in 1890 and 1907; enabling by-laws to be passed to improve the services of refuse collection. It did however neglect the other growing problem of commercial waste. This was partially rectified in 1891 when the Public Health (London) Act obligated local authorities to remove trade refuse on payment if required.

As the local councils became more organised, horse-drawn carts were sent on regular collection runs around the town as they picked up waste from households or accumulations on street corners. These would be - as today - on a specific day of the week or perhaps fortnightly. The human waste or sewerage gradually began to be filtered and treated in special 'farms' prior to its disposal into the rivers, seas and lakes. Toilets and garden sewage pits (cesspits) would be emptied into specially adapted tanker vehicles, which would also discharge at the sewerage farms. Solid waste gradually came under a weekly collection system, effectively sanitising the towns on a regular basis.

The next major milestone was not a Government Act but the formation of the Institute of Cleansing Superintendents in 1898. This organisation did wonders in promoting the improvements in refuse collection over the ensuing years and is still with us today in the guise of the Institute of Wastes Management with its head office in Northampton. The 1936 Public Health Act was inspired following an investigation by Mr. J. C. Dawes after continuous complaints about public cleansing in South London. The act brought in segregation of refuse collection allowing local authorities to charge for the disposal of certain types of waste.

The aforementioned midden or netty system lasted for centuries in some form or another, but increases in living standards saw the introduction of the 'privy', followed by the pail closet and water closet. Waste for the midden pile, instead of just being thrown out the back was eventually placed into a container that the refuse collectors then disposed of in the vehicle. This factor became the most noticeable and lasting legacy of the 1936 Act, which required the 'Introduction of a standard receptacle for temporary waste storage within a private residence'.

In other words it invented the Dustbin! Eventually this resulted in a British Standard (Number 792) for galvanised bins with new designs for kitchen and dustless loading bins (and subsequently plastic types). It is interesting to note that even in the 1970s despite the Act there were still rural areas in mainland Britain that utilised the individual's own containers because the standard dustbin system had not been implemented.

Other Acts beyond the scope of this book have influenced and changed our thinking and ways and no doubt will continue to cope with the ever-increasing amount of refuse we all throw out. The Local Authorities (Charges for Dustbins) Order 1959 continued this procedure by standardising bins in any given authority. Further Acts in 1961 and 1963 encompassed Factories, Shops, Offices and Railway premises. Also in 1963 The Ministry of Health set up a working party to examine Refuse Collection, this culminated in a report in 1967 which made extensive recommendations on the operation, funding and administration of refuse collection.

This examination was so thorough that it even examined large quantities of refuse itself, to establish that between the 1930s and 1950s there had been a considerable drop in the weight of refuse collected. This decrease continued as we gradually increased the usage of central heating and did away with coal fires.

SAMPLE RESULTS OF DUSTBIN CONTENTS (%)

	1933	1967	1992
FINES (inc. ash)	56.9	21.9	3.9
PUTRESCIBLES	13.7	17.6	32.0
PAPER/CARDBOARD	14.3	36.9	29.0
METALS	4.0	8.9	6.2
TEXTILES	1.9	2.4	3.0
GLASS	3.4	9.1	7.3
PLASTIC	nil	1.1	10.1
MISC	5.8	2.1	8.5

All figures are of weight, not volume.
The above information is received with thanks from The Institute of Wastes Management.

However the bulkiness of refuse increased alarmingly over the same period. Printing grew more elaborate and hence attractively packaged goods sold well. So, graced with greater affluence we threw more things away instead of 'making do' or repairing. Actually this phenomenon has only slowed in the 1990s, as we become more aware of our environment. In the 1950s and 1960s modern materials enabled more DIY work to be carried out at home so old cupboards, beds and other types of furniture were discarded like never before. As the collection vehicles of the day could not easily take this type of refuse, society went back to the old ways of throwing it out on the street, more often than not in the hedgerows and lanes of the nearby countryside.To combat this, in 1967 the Civic Amenities Act allowed local authorities to provide areas for the public to take their bulky refuse rather than dump it in the country. By providing these controlled sites free of charge, practices such as fly-tipping and abandoning cars were also largely wiped out.

Factory waste had its own problems; the sheer amount produced on any one site deemed the humble dustbin totally unacceptable. Larger bins were needed but as the operators obviously could not lift them, methods of getting these bigger bins to the vehicle had to be devised.

Above: *Standardisation of containers (bins) brought common order to the job, and in this 1950s view shop refuse is being loaded into one of Manchester's S&D side-loaders. Adjacent to the model TW vehicles the camera captures other scenes from the past including a delivery bicycle with a wicker basket, and Will's Woodbines cigarette sign above a vending machine.* Bob Whewell

Below: *As shops and factories grew, larger types of bins were needed, so the Paladin was adopted as the industrial standard. Here, in 1967, an eleptical sided bin is being demonstrated as it is tipped in to a Glover & Webb body fitted on to a Bedford TK chassis with a Reeves Crew Cab.* Vauxhall Motors Ltd.

Thus came about the bulk bin fitted with wheels or casters, a wonderful idea except when confronted with cobbled streets! Lifting these into the hopper meant more equipment had to be hung on the back of the vehicle; in turn, this would usually get right in the way of manual loading as it reduced the aperture at the back by over 50% in some cases. As a result special 'Bin-lifting vehicles had to be introduced to concentrate on the collection of industrial waste. Where this wasn't practical some manufacturers made their bin-lifting equipment removable so that it could be raised up above the loading area when not required. A further alternative was to equip the bin-lift with 'quick - release' hydraulic couplings in order that it may be removed on some days and quickly refitted as required.

Again a standard was desperately called for, as the vehicle manufacturers simply could not cope with having to provide equipment to lift every type of waste container then in use. This operational necessity led to the introduction of the Paladin bin, a tall round bin of galvanised steel that held a considerable amount of refuse and could weigh up to a ton when full. They had their drawbacks though, and being mounted on casters they were too high to load into easily, very unstable and could easily topple over. Furthermore, it was not unusual to see a full Paladin bin running away down a street or yard with two or three loaders in hot pursuit! Yet despite these faults they lasted for years until the 1980s when plastic once again paved the way for newer, more stable types of bulk bin with lower loading heights.

Top: *The large elipitical bins that were used for factories, shops, flats and tenements were, of course beyond the lifting capability of the loaders, and a means of movement and emptying had to be devised. Many bins were fitted with in-built casters and thus could be pushed to and from the refuse collection vehicles. Other authorities adopted small-wheeled trolleys to do the job, and these were usually stowed on the vehicles as they went along their rounds. Mechanical loading into the vehicles was another problem that had to be overcome, and due to the configuration of the Fore & Aft vehicles then in vogue, it was not possible to discharge a bulk bin with the body in its travelling position. To resolve this the bin would be clamped in place, and the body rotated to an upright position. This impressive view shows a Dennis Tippax from Guildford Corporation, with a bulk bin attached. Note the complicated cantilevered hydraulic pipe support arms, as well as the lugs for rear tipping and the bin lifting ram.* Londonderry Garage

Left: *A Northern Coachbuilders conversion of a Pagefield chassis for Sheffield City Council, tipping a bulk bin outside a block of flats on 26th June 1956. In order to accommodate the new standard bulk bins, each manufacturer had to devise its own equipment to attach it to the rear of the vehicle. Once this bin has been emptied into the body, the refuse would be dragged forward by scuppers, as described on pages 45-6. Note the speed limit plate of 20mph at the rear of the vehicle.* Sheffield City Council

STORAGE AND COLLECTION METHODS

To understand how the refuse collection vehicle evolved, we need to first understand the various ways in which refuse has been collected over the past century. Once the midden syndrome had been disposed of (pun not intended) and containers were the 'in thing', the method of transferring the full container from house, shops and factories to the collection vehicle had to be considered.

This was no light or easy matter, as the removal of refuse is a very complicated operation. Over the years many systems and methods were tried, and the vehicles employed were designed to reflect the methods used. Primarily these methods were introduced to improve efficiency and make the loaders' life easier, but as time went by it became equally important to compact more waste into the body or to mechanically discharge certain types of bin. In some brave cases, the vehicle manufacturers produced a new model with it's own bin system as well, but these didn't always work out.

The typecast image of the dustman at work is 'back door collection', as he walks to the rear of the house he brings out a full bin on his shoulder, empties it and returns the bin to the rear of the premises. Four journeys for each property, two of which were totally unproductive. As a consequence other types of collection were tried over the years.

Above: *A pair of Bedford TJ chassis in the yard of Cheadle Rural District Council fitted with particular neat crew cabs and Chelsea-type bodies with salvage racks above. Obviously brand new, the pair are probably awaiting inspection and approval by local councillors.* Vauxhall Motors Ltd.

One such method was 'collection and short return', which was much the same as the back door collection but in this the empty bin was left by the kerbside. Less walking for the bin-man but the householder had to take their soiled bin back to the property, albeit empty. Then there was the 'kerbside collection', which was very productive for the crew as there was very little walking involved. However, this was even more unpopular with the householders who had to move often quite heavy bins to the roadside.

The 'skep system' solved most of these problems, as the bin-man took his own container or skep to the rear of the house. Into this he tipped the refuse from the dustbin and carried it back to the vehicle, sometimes more than one dustbin could be emptied into the skep, further improving productivity. At back to back or terraced houses the men would often second an old pram, and this would be used to wheel their skep along the street loading a number of bins into it.

The obvious problem with this system was the frequent instances of transfer, with the possibility that either spillage or wind blown ash and paper could cause litter in the immediate vicinity. Another short-lived method was the 'dustbin exchange system', where the men started their round with an empty bin. At their first call of the morning they picked up the householder's full bin and left the empty one, the first bin would be emptied into the collection vehicle, and this was then deposited empty at the second house, and so on. This system was on a hiding to nothing from the very start as the householder at number 16 immediately objected to having number 14's bin! Even when vehicles were fitted with special bin-washing equipment there was still dissension and the system didn't last. Another method was 'wall mounted bins' which were seen mainly in the North. Here the bin was fixed to the wall of the house and could either be swivelled to discharge into a skep or detached and taken to the vehicle in the conventional way.

Another idea was the 'dustless loading system' that came across from Europe where it had been common in the 1930s, but did not make a major impact here until the late 1950s. This system became the forerunner of the modern wheeled bin system whereby the authority either supplied householders with lidded bins with wheels or gave their collection men wheeled trolleys to move ordinary bins. On arrival at the collection vehicle a mechanism, employing either hydraulic apparatus or cables at the rear, picked up the bin and sealed it against the aperture prior to allowing the lid to open for discharge. Most of these systems are illustrated in our photographs.

In later years and beyond the remit of this edition came the introduction of the paper sack system, followed by plastic sacks. The disadvantages of these systems were many; bags splitting; animals chewing through them; glass or jagged tin lids poked through, cutting loaders hands or legs; bottoms often fell out just as they were being thrown into the vehicle; bags being pinched. Some bag methods had special wired wall-mounted containers at the house, others required the householder to fit the bag into their existing dustbin. Trying to educate people to tie the bags each week was just another hopeless aspect of this method. Then there was the cost of the bags! Although many authorities still employ the sack collection method, the wheeled bin now seems to be the accepted universal method of collecting and disposing of refuse today - that is until someone comes up with yet another method!

Top: *An Edison Electricar with a raised cover and dust shield, is seen being loaded from a 'skep' with a rather ornate dust cover c1920.* Sheffield City Council
Centre: *Several manufacturers developed a treadle system for operating dust covers on the body, as for example this type fitted to a Garner RW3 with Brentwood UDC.* Anthony Thomas
Bottom: *A Shefflex dustless loading system showing the control handle on the body side at the rear, and the wire-guided pulley system that lifted the bins to the top of the body.* Sheffield City Council.

HORSEPOWER!

Horses and donkeys were the accepted mode of power up to the late-19th Century. As the collection of midden piles became more widespread, so these beasts were engaged to pull all manner of carts around by the local waste collectors and transport the waste to some convenient hole nearby. Following the 1875 Act local authorities literally took up the reins and developed carts for the specific use of refuse collection. Even then there was the need to load as much as possible into the cart prior to going to the tip, which was usually an old worked out quarry or natural hole in the vicinity of the town. This posed several problems; to start with a horse drawn cart has to have a high floor level for the front (turning) wheels to pass underneath; this meant difficulties for the loaders in emptying the containers, even from off the shoulder. Drop down sides and tail-boards helped for the first part of the load, but once the refuse was up to the top of the lower section there was nothing for it but to put the sides up and get out the ladders! The men then climbed up the ladder to tip the refuse in! Health and Safety Officers, had there been any in those times, would have had a field day!

The carts were 'modernised' by some enterprising authorities who installed screw tipping gear as the alternative to shovelling the refuse out at the tip! Canvas covers were added to reduce dust nuisance and smells. Horse-drawn refuse carts were with us right up to the 1930s and in some areas they were still operational after World War II. But before the turn of the century the writing was on the wall for the horse. The scene was set for the next phase of progress!

Above: *This splendid horse-drawn rig originally operated in Southampton, and was one of the last of its type in service. It was discovered in a derelict condition in Reading, but has since been restored by Grundon's. Behind is the firm's restored Albion side-loader, whilst towering above the horses is one of the new Grundon container loaders on an ERF chassis.* S. Grundon Services Ltd.

Below: *Is this the first recorded dustcart parade? Here messrs Stone and Schofield pause with their donkey 'Cloe' and an immaculate cart at an unrecorded event.* Sheffield City Council

THE FIRST MECHANISED VEHICLES

It was on the very eve of the 19th century that motorised refuse collection vehicles received their first major endorsement, and thus this book now marks the centenary of a significant event. This event came at the annual conference of The Cleansing Superintendents of Great Britain assembled in Glasgow on 7th September 1899, when it was declared that those gathered there were:

'Of the opinion that recent developments in the construction of motor vehicles justifies the gradual introduction of self-propelled vehicles in several branches of cleansing operations and this meeting recommends Municipal, Urban and other Authorities to take the question in their serious consideration.' Therefore, towards the latter part of the 19th-century mechanised transport was slowly beginning to spread around the more wealthy sections of the populace.

Above: *Electric refuse vehicles came in an amazing array of designs ranging from the slab fronted, gruesome-looking Garretts, through the rather comical Edisons and tiny 3-wheelers, to the rather elegant Ransome models. Here a brand new unit is displayed outside the Ransomes works prior to its delivery to Newport Corporation Scavenging Dept.* Rural History Centre, University of Reading

It quickly became apparent also that the internal combustion engine was a lot more powerful than the lowly horse. However, although petrol-driven open trucks and vans were produced to carry all manner of goods including refuse, they were very basic and unreliable. Liquid sewage had to wait a while for technology to find a way of keeping the offending slurry from spilling all over the place.

For a period of time some enterprising local authorities worked the horse hand in hand with the new trucks, using horse-drawn carts for collection and motor lorries for disposal. The horse-drawn cart with its limited capacity and speed would, when full, progress to a certain street corner or other pre-determined spot whereupon the mechanised truck would converge. When the two came together, the lorry would lower either a demountable body or containers to the ground with manpower and cables. At the same time as these empty containers were being lowered, a similar operation would occur to the full body behind the horse. Once completed, the truck would then uplift the full body or container taking it away to the tip and the horse would be led back to continue on the round. By this method one truck could service a number of horse-drawn vehicles allowing them to continue collecting without wasting time travelling to and from the tip. Several makers tried this arrangement, including Pagefield.

Some authorities also tried 'external' combustion engines, either in the form of steam waggons or traction engines towing carts. These were a hopeless case from the start. Traction engines were very expensive (both to purchase and run), whilst their poor manoeuvrability did not suit the narrow places in which they were generally employed. They also caused a not inconsiderable level of nuisance by smoke and noise, which often frightened the other horse drawn traffic or belched soot on to the lines of washing strung between terraced houses! Steam waggons were little better, although their compound engines were quieter than traction engines. Whilst the boilers were usually in the cabs, the engines of steam waggons were under-slung, and by virtue of this their bodies had very high loading levels as well as restricted payloads. Whilst having the body on the waggon rather than towing a cart was an improvement on the steam traction engine, manoeuvrability was still a further serious disadvantage.

Top: *The City of Birmingham was a major user of electric traction for its refuse collection services, and the last of the type remained in service until 1971. This GV Electric, seen in 1931 (probably just after delivery) was just one of the many types operated. Almost all the electric vehicle manufacturers had machines in service with this authority at some time or another.* Birmingham & Midland Motor Omnibus Trust

Centre: *Another idea to oust horses from collection work was the introduction of steam traction, but it really never worked. One of the authorities to try this method was Walthamstow UDC, and their Clayton 'Overtype' is seen here in Edward Road. The awkwardness of the loading height is amply illustrated.* Vestry House Museum

Bottom: *In order to prove their products, demonstration units were built by most manufacturers and taken around the various local authorities. This AEC, complete with 'crew-cab' is fitted with an Eagle rotating body designed to compress and pulverise the load and thus reduce runs to the tip.* Sheffield City Council

Above: *A Garrett 5-ton 'Overtype' steam waggon built in 1921 for the Corporation of Chatham, with the works number 34073 and registered number KE 4508. It is fitted with canvas top covers on a removable frame with drop-down sides and has mechanical tipping.* Suffolk Records Office

Below: *Tips have been the enemy of the refuse vehicle for many years and this Bedford TK shows a typical problem as its front end has 'lifted' whilst attempting to discharge its load from its Eagle Crushload body. As will be seen the heavy compactor section could rise to a considerable height, and as such the centre of gravity shifted and the vehicles suffered varying degrees of instability or balance. At times this could (and did) have dire consequences on rough tips where the ground beneath an axle or wheel might suddenly give way.* Vauxhall Motors Ltd.

However, one local authority did report that 'Each of our Steamers saved £175.00 per annum when it replaced the horse and cart on collection work.' Calculations also showed that one steam waggon could do the work of six horse and cart combinations. Several authorities were proud of their 'steamers'; Chelsea for instance boasted about its fleet of 15 Leyland steam-powered tippers which carried the 'Noah's Ark' type body. These bodies were so named after their shape, which, above wooden slatted sides rose to an apex along the centre-line of the vehicle giving the impression of the 'Ark'. Both Westminster and Chiswick ran Thornycroft steam collection vehicles, but it seems that only the better off authorities could afford to engage in experiments with steam.

In the end petrol engined vehicles won the day, for they were far lighter and more manoeuvrable. Even so, reliability was the big problem throughout the first two decades of the 20th-century. The limited choice of proprietary vehicles then available stood little chance of handling the arduous stop - start work, dusty atmosphere and rough tips that were both common at the time and indeed indicative of refuse collection.

The other method of gas combustion, was brought about by necessity during World War I. At this time a large number of vehicles were thus converted and were equipped with robust inflatable bags on top to contain the gas. In World War II the London Borough of Croydon went one step further and ran a Guy 'Vixen' 4-ton tipper on compressed methane produced from sewage. Bradford tried this type of re-cycling in conjunction with a local car manufacturer, Jowetts, who converted council cars and vans to run on gas!

The manner of loading refuse into the collection vehicle has been virtually unchanged from the days of the horse and cart down to today; you pick it up in a container and throw the contents in. Getting it back out again at the landfill site was a different matter and this is where the greatest innovations were needed. In this respect it was quickly realised that, having been disturbed from it's cosy resting place where the matter may have been quietly festering for some time, the process of shovelling it off the truck at the tip was a particularly unpleasant and smelly task! So methods of discharge were devised using tipping techniques.

Originally a hand-driven or mechanical screw threaded pole would be rotated to raise the front of the body, the rear being held on two swivel points. Ingenious cable systems were also used by certain manufacturers as part of the tipping process, and some of these manufacturers also employed cables to synchronise the raising of the tailgate with the lifting of the body. As the streets were tidied up and the towns began to smell healthier it was realised that the open 'dustcart' as it was now known was becoming a major cause of smells itself! Lids were the answer and so by the turn of the century the specialised refuse collection vehicle had finally arrived.

As local authorities had a mandate to collect refuse, there was suddenly a very large market for RCV's all over the country. A number of manufacturers sprang up in rapid succession about this time, including Dennis, Lacre and Shelvoke & Drewry.

Whilst production at these firms soon became rapid, the actual delivery of the vehicles to council depots was far from swift, especially those that were located some distance from the vehicle manufacturers. The early trucks had solid tyres, some on wheels only 20 inches in diameter, and these were not designed for travelling long distance journeys.

Crude unreliable petrol engines, basic gearing and top speeds of 10 - 15 mph were about as much as you could expect. That's all very well when trundling along the collection rounds but delivering a vehicle, say from Letchworth to Newcastle, on roads which were often un-metalled, and in a cab that consisted of only a roof was a very long and uncomfortable job! Indeed it could take several days to deliver a brand new dustcart, but it was certainly run-in on arrival!

This delivery journey was normally the longest the vehicle would ever undertake, (many of course went by rail where convenient) and at the end of its life the furthest it usually went was the local scrap merchants!

Above: *To emphasise the comment opposite, in 1985 Norba found a derelict RCV in a Swedish scrap-yard. Mounted on a Volvo Penta bus chassis, the body was fitted with an air-operated dustless loading system and of some historical significance. It had been built in 1937, and then delivered from the factory at Kalmar (in the south-east of the country) by rail to Gothenburg where it worked for some 40 years before being discarded. Norba recovered it by low-loader, and after complete restoration it was decided that its first public display would be at an important exhibition in Britain. So it was sent back to Gothenburg by low-loader, and then sent via sea to Felixstowe. Once it arrived a colleague and I duly collected it from the docks with the intention of driving it to London, as it was due to take part in the London to Brighton Commercial Vehicle Rally prior to the exhibition. This drive to London was the longest trip the vehicle had ever done in the whole of its forty-odd years, maybe that's why it caught fire along the A12! Help was summoned in the form of a suspended tow to a north London garage at 60 miles an hour! (No doubt the fastest it had ever travelled as well!). The damage was in effect quite minor and following the fitting of a new Leyland fan-belt and after some tidying up it successfully managed both the rally and the exhibition!*

Above: This 1930s Dennis-Eagle illustrates the type of vehicle referred to in the text opposite, and has a specially adapted Dennis chassis and a reduced frame height to ease loading. The rollers and cogs of the rotating body are clearly seen, as are the bump-stops to prevent overturning. The screw tipping gear can be seen above the vehicle's crew/salvage locker behind the cab, which has the tipping control besides it. Sheffield City Council

Below: This Bedford O type is equipped with an Eagle 'Chelsea' body and salvage rack above. Of interest is the special Enid lift developed for use with container work in the Borough of Bermondsey, which obviously reduced manual handling of bulk bins. This type of lorry-mounted crane has been significantly developed in recent years, but not on refuse vehicles. Vauxhall Motors Ltd.

Problems of delivery aside, the refuse collection vehicle market rapidly evolved with numerous manufacturers trying to outdo each other with innovations aimed to tempt the buyers, usually local authority committees. As more and more authorities turned to mechanisation, many adopted the new S&D Freighter with it's low loading height and simplicity. The concept was rapidly copied by others including the somewhat unlikely Guy and Vulcan vehicles, and also the lesser-known Carrimore, Dearne and Lowtruck. Dennis and Karrier were the more successful in this field although Pagefield had considerable achievements in the early years. All manner of ideas were tried including hydraulic tipping, sliding lids, automatic tailgates, moving floors, dustless loading, larger bodies, demountable pods and bodies, weather-proof cabs, gearbox PTOs, pneumatic tyres, crew cabs, diesel engines and ignition key starting.

Some of the ideas were if anything a little too ambitious to say the least, as for example the Eagle dustless loader. This featured a revolving tank-like body with four filling apertures, which exactly fitted the rims of the upturned dustbins, but only providing you used the Eagle type of bin! Rotation of the tank gave a little compression to the load and it tipped for discharge. Another novel idea from Eagle was an articulated trailer fitted with a rotating frame on which empty dustbins were hung, these were used in the 'Exchange Method' where empty bins were swapped for full ones. By rotating the frame each row of bins became available for swapping, and when they were all full the vehicle went off to the tip where it must have been fun emptying the bins one by one!

In 1930, the chassis manufacturer Karrier built their own type of dustless body using German equipment built under licence. This appeared very tidy and modern with the body blending in with the cab. Just behind the cab was an aperture into which the refuse was discharged, whilst the body featured a rotor which threw the refuse to the rear therefore again giving some measure of compaction. Then, at the tip this rotor also aided discharge.

Ideas came and went, but one system, the 'side-loader', was to prove its value above all the others. There were three basic types, Chelsea, Derby and Newcastle (named after the authorities that introduced them) but all served a similar function.The sheer simplicity of the system with its 'chip-pan' lids ensured that it was to outlast many of the more complex earlier ideas. Indeed not until the 'rear-end loader' was introduced did the death knell toll for the humble side loader.

Even then several authorities kept the side-loader for certain jobs, especially those where its simple efficiency could not be bettered by more technically developed vehicles. An example would be in municipal parks or along sea front promenades. In fact anywhere where load capacities were low, or where access was restricted. At the time of writing modern side loaders still work along Blackpool's Golden Mile. But in other places the new technology was applied and improvements made and, as the years went by, the vehicles became ever more complex.

First of all the improved steels used in manufacture both increased in strength and reduced the tare weight, thereby allowing bigger payloads. Then, during the 1960s, aluminium bodies were introduced offering further weight reductions. Next came new compaction techniques, although the early methods were somewhat crude and ineffective! One of these new methods was the 'Barrier Loader' system, which boasted a full width rear opening with wide steps to allow the operators to walk into the rear of the body and tip the bins' contents over a movable barrier. This barrier or partition was suspended on tracks and locked into position with spring bolts. At the start of the day the barrier began at the front of the body, but as refuse filled the initial small space so it was eased to the rear bit by bit. Compaction results varied and they often relied on the smallest member of the crew clambering over the barrier and doing a bit of heavy footwork! The secret of discharging these vehicles was a piece of rope brought into play to raise the barrier out of the way as the body was tipped.

The other system was the 'moving floor', which was initially developed by The Principality Wagon Company of Cardiff. They produced a body with a heavy-duty rubber floor that could be wound forward. Initially it was all done by hand, although it was eventually powered. This system allowed the loaders to simply tip the bins at the rear of the vehicle, after which the floor was wound forward taking the rubbish with it. Discharge was effected by reversing the floor movement, and whilst this was not a very rapid process it was considerably more stable than the tipping barrier loader. Several makers tried this system under licence from the Cardiff company.

Shelvoke & Drewry went one better with their 'Fore & Aft' tipper, which actually tipped the body up in the air whilst the vehicle was still on its rounds! Later models were offered with a compaction plate which, when the body was raised, was brought into action to compress the load. By this time all the ancillary equipment was driven hydraulically, usually via a power-take-off on the gearbox and this enabled further development of items like large bulk bins (Paladins) for industrial premises. The hydraulic operated clamps would engage the bin and lift it bodily to discharge into the body, alternatively with Fore & Aft wagons the whole body was rotated forwards into the vertical position with the bulk bin attached.

Mechanisation was certainly important, but so too were greater payloads. By this time many of the edge of town disposal sites had become filled up, and so the refuse had to be moved to new sites further out. This meant that to make effective use of the vehicles, every inch of space in them had to be used to maximum capacity. The clamour for better compaction was becoming significantly important, and side-loaders began giving way to the larger fore & aft tippers.

A method was obviously required to compress the refuse before it entered the body, so a system was devised whereby the refuse was emptied into a well at the rear of the vehicle. From there a hydraulic oscillating blade compressed the newly deposited rubbish into that which was already in the body.

Although the Fore & Aft tipper concept is synonymous with the firm of Shelvoke & Drewry, their first attempt at this design did not come about until 1949. On the other hand the Shefflex company introduced the first Fore & Aft tipper (pictured inset) around 1900. It had 6' diameter wheels, and thus the largest wheels of any refuse collection vehicle to date. Shefflex then went on to develop the principle for motor vehicles, and one such example is on this Electricar chassis supplied to Sheffield. As the picture below clearly shows, raising the body allowed the refuse to fall to the front of the body thus effecting 'gravity' compaction. However, a few incidents in operation showed that care was needed to ensure there were no power cables or telegraph wires around at the time! (Especially if you had a Paladin bin on as well!) Sheffield City Council

Above: *As described in the text, the compression type vehicles were exceptionally popular, and over the years they were produced by several manufacturers. The various vehicle models that were built had appropriate colloquialisms such as Pakmaster, Paxit and Pakamatic. This Dennis Paxit supplied to the City Of Westminster typifies the new regime of the 1950s and '60s, as the builders went over to aluminium bodies in order to reduce weight, increase payloads and minimise the effects of corrosion.*

Below: *This 1958 view of an Albion Chieftain shows the potential danger of a jammed load in a transfer or incineration stations, such as this one in Glasgow. Jerking the vehicle forward on the clutch could help, but if not judged correctly it could also cause the front end to lift to cause the rear end to drop in to the pit. In this case the Gibson Pendulum body has successfully discharged its load. The twin tipping rams were a factor in this model's stability.*
Biggar Museum Trust

Initially, the compaction on these 'compression' types was slight or even non-existent at the start of the round, but as the body filled so the compression increased. The vehicle was declared full when it reached the maximum pressure set by the hydraulics so that the blade would push no more and the blow-off valve dumped the hydraulic oil back to the tank. This system, although solving the difficulties of poor loading, created a further problem of how to move the compaction system out of the way when the vehicles were discharging their loads at the tip.

The solution was found when a technique was devised by which the body could be split, so that when tipping commenced the rear half containing the compactor was cantilevered out and upwards into the air above the body. This allowed the refuse to discharge underneath, and its effectiveness persuaded several manufacturers to follow this principle for many years. It was a major step in the evolution of the refuse collection vehicle, but it was still fraught with danger as a heavily compacted load could easily stick in the body and cause all manner of difficulties. The other problem was that the vehicle could tip backwards, lifting the cab high into the air.

Horizontal ejection discharge reduced these factors as the body was rigidly fixed to the chassis and only the rear compacting section was lifted. The Ejection Plate then moved to the rear, hydraulically pushing the refuse in front of it and thereby effecting discharge. The added benefit was that the Ejection Plate could be positioned to the rear of the body prior to loading thereby increasing the compaction rate much earlier in the loading cycle.

One drawback to this was that very soon after loading had commenced the vehicle could be overloaded on its rear axle for some time. This situation was only rectified when the compacted refuse built up against the plate which then eased forward, thus transferring more of the weight to the front axle and making the vehicle legal again! Although it took 10 years to effect, the days of the tipper were numbered and eventually all the manufacturers turned to ejection discharge. Several firms produced the packing blade system of compaction in various forms, but it was not totally universal!

Glover Webb & Liversidge from the Old Kent Road, and Norba both produced a screw-feed compacting system. In this system a large carbon-steel screw was built into the rear portion of the body, and this featured a reducing pitch and breadth which pulverised the refuse and compacted it. This gave a very high degree of compression and in turn this allowed a smaller, and therefore lighter body. Hence this gave a better payload and was very successful.

Laird of Anglesey produced a rear-loading body that compressed the refuse in a large rotating drum. Continuous loading compaction machines all had one big problem - wear! Even the modern steels and aluminium could not withstand the constant grinding of the load. Continuous loading also contributed to noise in the street and therefore intermittent loading was tried. In this process 10 - 15 bins would be loaded into the rear hopper, before a large plate would sweep the load into the body. This was the forerunner of all modern refuse vehicles but it is beyond the remit of this present book!

ELECTRICARS L?

CITY OF SHEFFIELD

CLEANSING DEPT.

WE 400

Above: *This delightful 30cwt Electricar demonstrates some of the comforts given to crews in 1926. A virtually full cab and side sheets offer some protection to both the men and the batteries (the latter being located under the cab seats).* Sheffield City Council

We always expect the 'dustman' to come on a certain day of the week, but what about the panic we get into if he doesn't arrive at the appointed time? We generally take the whole thing for granted with no thought to the vast industry that operates to ensure he does arrive when we expect him. Due to the type of job it is, i.e. unskilled, dirty, menial and laborious, it historically attracted the less ambitious members of our society and in consequence was often frowned upon by the rest of us.

Today however this has all been transformed, partly due to the change in the refuse itself, which is now far lighter and cleaner than it used to be. There is also the new technology which requires the modern refuse collection operatives to master the intricacies of quite complicated hydraulics whilst discharging the refuse into the vehicle. Added to this is the appearance of the operators who now usually wear high-tec protective clothing, which looks bright and smart despite the dirty nature of the job. With the arrival of uniforms and protective 'gear', gone are the days of the tatty ragged clothes portrayed in Lonnie Donnegan's pop song 'My Old Man's A Dustman'.

Traditionally this was always a hard job, the refuse was heavy, dirty, smelly, dusty and in general probably one of the most unpleasant products that man had to handle. The dustmen in consequence looked dirty and, after a hard day's work, smelt much like the refuse themselves. Hot ashes could fall on the men, soot would fly all over the place, and it was not uncommon for rats to jump out of the back of the vehicle as the bin was emptied. Mind you this latter hazard was often turned into an amusing diversion by the dustmen as they chased the offending rodent down the street hoping to effect revenge with a size ten boot! Often bins, when hoisted on to the shoulder, would leak. Quite what came out of the bins, no one dared think. When emptying them into the vehicle glass might fly in all directions. Then, in later years (when the familiar black plastic bag became popular), broken glass became a very serious problem.

It was a poorly paid job that had to be done whatever the weather, and the hours were often intolerably long. Toilet functions had to be improvised where and when the need required it! There was nowhere to wash their hands, except a roadside puddle (or if they were lucky an outside tap). Then they had to eat their lunch in the vehicle's cab, not pleasant on a wet day when there was no alternative but to sit there in sodden clothes.

Initially when horse-drawn collections first began just two men would go out on the rounds, but as the population grew and mechanised refuse vehicles came in (and the bodies on them became larger than a horse could handle) the requirement for more men became apparent. The rounds also became too long for the crew to walk alongside the vehicle which, incidentally, could now travel faster anyway. So the crew cab was born, this developed to its ultimate size in the 1970s where up to six loaders could be accommodated.

This meant that comparatively huge tonnages could now be handled in a day's work. Where the horse drawn vehicle might only manage two $1/2$-ton or $3/4$-ton loads each day at the turn of the century, by the 1970s in dense urban environments with a short run to the tip a six-man crew plus driver could handle between 35 and 40 tons. Technology introduced in the last two decades has however reversed the situation with regard to manpower, in as much that in the 1990s with the various hydraulic loading systems that are now available, crews are often now back to just two or three men.

Top: *What happens when the bin-man does not call. This picture is typical of the situation in many residential areas after a Bank Holiday, or worse still - a strike. Every bin is overflowing, lids are missing, boxes are piled on top and refuse is strewn around the street. In these situations, not only were the bins far heavier than normal, but the vehicle would become full much sooner, and extra trips to the tip would be needed.* Sheffield City Council

Centre: *How to demonstrate your new crew cab! This heavily modified Bedford had a forward tilt cab giving excellent access to the engine, but the method of propping the cab is not so impressive. To have a driver and five loaders on a relatively low-capacity side loader must have resulted in quite a number of trips to the tip each day.* Vauxhall Motors Ltd

Bottom: *The City Of Leeds Cleansing Department ran a huge fleet of refuse vehicles, and it placed much of its business for the early mechanised vehicles with the manufacturer Karrier Motors in nearby Huddersfield. It stuck with its loyalty to this maker after its takeover by Commer Motors (which then became part of the Rootes Group), and this is seen in this 1962 view of two new Karrier Gamecocks. Fitted with Glover & Webb bodies, crew cabs and Perkins diesel engines, this pair have registration numbers 882 CUA and 884 CUA.* H S Transport Collection

FIRE AND OTHER HAZARDS

Refuse vehicles are, by virtue of their being, highly dangerous pieces of equipment. Because of the necessity to retain mobility, the normal safety rules and regulations imposed (latterly by the Health & Safety Executive) are very difficult to enforce. The restrictive nature of the vehicle, (i.e. it must comply with road safety legislation) means that safety guards and interlocking safety mechanisms are difficult (if not impossible) to fit, and compromises have had to be reached. Furthermore, the fact that the vehicle is constantly changing its location also means that enforcement of any safety regulations is severely hampered.

Sadly it is human nature to find a quicker way to do something even if it is not the safest way. A classic example of dangerous working in the old days, was that crews often used to travel on the rear of the vehicle rather than walk alongside it as they were supposed to do. So, to stop the obvious problems this caused (i.e. falling off the vehicle when it was moving) steps or platforms were provided for the men. Yet even this presented further dangers especially when vehicles behind ran into the loaders standing on the back, or if the refuse vehicle pulled away sharply and threw the men into the path of a following vehicle. The worst consequence of this practice was found if the RCV driver braked sharply, as this could catapult the loaders into the rear hopper. It takes little imagination to understand the results that could (and did) happen when the crushing or compacting gear was operating at the same time!

Above: *The advent of rear loading steps, such as these on this Albion belonging to Glasgow Corporation, was welcomed by the collectors. However, the use of them for riding invariably ended in trouble. A spate of injury problems led to the steps being removed, but as old habits die hard, some of the loaders would then sit on the loading rave bar whilst on their rounds. Others would hang on to any protuberances from the rear of the vehicle, so if anything the problem was compounded. A threat of instant dismissal for any operative seen riding on the back eventually resolved the situation, but a few still took silly chances.* Biggar Museum Trust

When tipping bins into the back of the RCV, fingers, gloves or clothing could get caught and the unfortunate man could get dragged into the packing mechanism. Alternatively, the bin itself would sometimes be caught by the packing mechanism, invariably the man concerned would try to retrieve it again but with dire consequences on some occasions. This sort of thing has happened on several occasions, but no one else has realised an accident has sadly taken place. In some recorded instances it was even presumed by the rest of the crew that the man had absconded, and the misapprehension was not corrected until the gruesome remains were discharged with the rest of the load at the tip! It was not safe back in the workshops either, as maintenance men were always at particular risk when clambering about in the rear of a vehicle.

Above: *It is quite clear from this picture how the stability of a vehicle altered when tipping, for not only does the weight of the hopper and packing mechanism come into the equation, but so too did the variable weight of the load of refuse. This Albion with a Gibson body has just been washed at one of Glasgow Corporation's depots, and it has been left to drip-dry. Washing was usually done by means of a hose and a long brush.* Biggar Museum Trust

Below: *Pictures of dustbin men climbing ladders to empty bins into horse-drawn carts are not all that common, but this 1948 view shows that the arduous practice was still continuing after World War II, at least in the London Borough of St. Pancras. Here an operative empties a 'pig-swill' bin into a Bedford OST tipper lorry with extended side boards that bear the legend Waste Food Collection. It is almost inconceivable today that such techniques, with all the attendant dangers, were still being employed.*

Fire was a further serious hazard. I say 'was' as in today's modern society few of us have coal fires any more, and it was the disposal of hot ashes into the bin that inevitably caused the fire problem. The bin with the hot embers would be emptied into the hopper unnoticed along with wood, paper and other flammable materials from neighbouring bins. Gradually in the protected, compacted environment of the collection vehicle's body, the fire would take hold.

A mad dash to the tip would ensue, with smoke and flames billowing from the rear of the vehicle. At the tip the fire brigade would be called to effect a solution to the situation. In one or two cases bin men are recorded to have actually driven their vehicle straight to the nearest fire station for the flames to be extinguished. After one of these incidents, in which a 'dustcart' tipped its burning load in to a fire station yard, a fireman commented that 'in 23 years it was the first time anyone had brought the fire to him!' I dread to think what was said about the inevitable mess that remained.

However, despite the amusing sight this may have conveyed to onlookers, the consequences for the vehicle were quite serious. The heat would no doubt have caused distortion to its body and the hydraulic hoses would have easily perished, in a worst case scenario the vehicle may have to be abandoned en-route. Depot fires were not uncommon, especially when a vehicle had not been cleaned out or tipped perhaps through a fault. If slow combustion had set in within the load, the vehicle could suddenly reach a critical point where it broke into flames.

Not only would this have consequential damage to the vehicle itself, but it could also affect the empty vehicles parked nearby. It is not unknown for vehicle fires in depots to have destroyed large proportions of a local authority fleet overnight. One such example was at Colchester back in 1976, when a vehicle was not tipped due to a mechanical problem. During the night spontaneous combustion occurred in the load, and the vehicle caught fire. By the time the fire brigade had been alerted, some seven vehicles had been rendered completely or partially burnt out. Other incidents occurred when cables snapped during tipping, thus causing the vehicle to turn over. Hydraulic hoses have burst whilst packing, spraying hydraulic oil all over the place; and when this occurred in a busy shopping centre the mess and confusion had to be seen to be believed. Fortunately, these are now things of the past as today's modern vehicles have brake valves which, when there is a sudden loss of pressure, close and thereby prevent all but the smallest amount of oil spillage.

The nature of the driving of a refuse vehicle, in and out of very tight spaces and corners (for example down back alleys, behind shops, into factories etc.) inevitably leads to scrapes and bangs. In the days of tippers it was not unknown for a driver to leave the tip forgetting to let down his body. Whilst the tearing down of a few telegraph wires may have gone unnoticed, the consequence of trying to negotiate the first low bridge with a raised body could cause severe problems! At the point of collision the body stopped abruptly thereby halting the vehicle and shooting the cab up into the underside of the bridge, again with horrific consequences.

Above: *Where conventional landfill sites were unavailable, other methods of discharge were used. These 'transfer stations' were usually constructed on permanent sites, using a hard standing in order to reduce wear and tear on the vehicles. Transfer stations came in all manner of guises, and here we see one with a pair of Lambeth Borough Council Dennis PAX vehicles, with barrier loading bodies, discharging refuse into Thames barges for disposal at a land reclamation site downstream.*

Because of the nature of the work i.e. stop - start all day long and rough riding over tips, the engines and tyres took a considerable hammering. So much so that many refuse vehicles had an 'Engine Hours' clock in the cab in order that servicing could be geared to the hours the engine was running rather than the mileage or time scales normally applied to other municipal vehicles.

Tyres were constantly being ripped apart on tips, and adhesion was often a problem with holes and bumps all over the place. In the days before top-soil was spread over the refuse, any driver who got stuck when trying to get out would invariably spin the rear wheels and these might well have landed on broken glass or sharp metal objects with the obvious consequences. Changing a tyre on a tip was not very practicable, apart from the obvious difficulties of unstable ground, the vehicle was probably in the way of others trying to discharge. Therefore the site's bulldozer would usually be brought over to drag the offending vehicle to one side where repairs could be safely effected.

Dust was the other major problem as ash and soot found its way into and onto every surface and crevice. A liberal coating of the stuff would materialise after just a couple of days service, and when this was mixed with a drop of hydraulic oil and a smattering of rain then you ended up with a wonderful concoction that literally glued itself to the vehicle. Dust penetrated filters; it got into joints and bearings; it covered the cab and dashboard; in fact it was everywhere. It was only after the introduction of effective steam cleaning apparatus that the service man's job became a more pleasant task.

It was not uncommon for crews to get into trouble on the rounds, as even residential areas presented their own particular type of problems. To illustrate this point I would refer to an incident that occurred whilst I was with Shelvoke's. This particular week I was demonstrating a TN Pakamatic for Brentwood Urban District Council, where I was being instructed to drive along a round by the local driver. This particular area had rather well-appointed houses set back about 50 to 60 yards from the road, so it meant that the bins had to be carried for quite some distance. Therefore, wherever there was turning space behind the houses, the practice was to take the vehicle down the driveway, load the refuse, turn and proceed back on to the road. One particular property was the local vicar's house, which was built in an 'L' shape, so once behind it you were invisible from the front.

Having driven down what looked like a nice new tarmac drive, I pulled up at the rear and duly reversed into the crux of the 'L' shaped property, only to have a sinking feeling come over me. The vehicle had gone down through the tarmac right up to its rear axle with the front wheels going in as well. By the time I stopped, the vehicle was leaning over and the top rear corner of the body was about two inches from puncturing the kitchen window! Fortunately nobody was home!

Help was needed, so one of the crew went off down the road and flagged down a local Highways Department lorry which they brought round the back of the house. The crews hitched a rope on to the front and tried to pull me clear. The lorry pulled and pulled, but to no avail, although it did make more mess of the tarmac!

A 'phone call then brought a 16-ton S&D Pakamatic to join the rescue. Although this was a much larger vehicle, I was fully loaded and thus weighed a lot more! Therefore I remained stuck fast, and the tarmac drive looked liked a ploughed field. Another SOS call eventually enlisted the services of a JCB digger, and after manoeuvring the other vehicles out of the way it was chained on to my front bumper. With very little effort, it proceeded to haul me out of the mire with its hydraulic bucket arm.

At this point we now had two S&D vehicles, a highways lorry and a JCB in the back garden plus about a dozen men! Having freed the vehicle, I clambered down from the cab, only to notice a car coming down the drive. It was the vicar! Seeing me he stopped, wound down the window surveyed the scene of utter destruction to his back yard and just said 'Oh my God' - but I wonder what he was really thinking?

THE UK MANUFACTURERS

Above: *In ex-works condition, this Dennis Tippax has probably been prepared for an exhibition prior to its delivery to Stoke-on-Trent. Note the attention to detail, including the way the name Firestone has been picked out in white paint on the tyres. This particular model came with either a side-valve petrol engine or a diesel engine.* Londonderry Garage

As previously mentioned, the life of a refuse vehicle is very arduous and quite unlike that faced by the average commercial vehicle chassis, on which most collection vehicle bodies were originally mounted. Before the introduction of special chassis, the whole machine would suffer from abnormal mechanical structural stresses, from both the stop-start actions on the round and afterwards on the rough ground at the tip.

Consequently production of these vehicles became a very specialised technique and although many companies tried their hands at the task few succeeded and the industry soon set itself apart from the general truck business. The companies that were successful governed the industry for many years. Dozens of companies became involved with this new market, but few actually made anything out of it. Consequently, many merged or were taken over as time went on, and even some of the so-called 'Big-Boys' have since succumbed.

The following alphabetic list gives an idea of some of the variety of organisations who produced complete vehicles; built specific chassis for the purpose; supplied components such as batteries and control equipment; fitted bodies to chassis; or in some cases specialised in fitting one company's bodies to another's chassis! Some companies just dabbled with refuse vehicles and quickly returned to their own specific area. Many other outfits, too numerous to list, were of course involved in various ways throughout the period covered by this book.

AEC (ASSOCIATED EQUIPMENT COMPANY),

This well-known company from Southall in Middlesex produced a number of early refuse vehicles, some in conjunction with Eagle. They later developed a heavily altered 'Monarch' chassis with Shefflex as part of the Sheffield bodybuilder's futuristic 'Ideal' dustless refuse collection system. But their strength lay in the conventional commercial market, and as several large companies invested strongly in AEC (as for example London Transport and London Brick) the supply of AEC chassis for refuse applications were generally few and far between. In all AEC supplied thousands of buses for use in London, and they also produced trolley buses, and diesel railcars for the Great Western Railway, so the humble dustcart did not figure strongly in their sales promotions.

Above: *Despite the factors mentioned opposite, AEC's experience in heavy vehicles did pay some small part in the refuse vehicle story as they built a fleet of 8 Mammoth Majors (7 of which are seen above) for a private haulage contractor (Pannell's). In turn this firm had a contract to transfer bulk waste from the London Borough of Lambeth to outlying landfill sites. Indeed, trans-shipment of refuse out of our major cities is nothing new and back in the 1950s, as can be seen on page 4, local council vehicles would bring in the rubbish to a central point. This was the Embankment Depot, where it was tipped on to the ground then, with the use of grab cranes, it was scooped up and dropped into the AEC Mammoth Majors (with opening roof bodies). Double handling of this type, whilst expensive kept the collection vehicles on the rounds, and the crews fully occupied. AEC*

ALBION MOTORS

With their slogan 'as sure as the sunrise', Albion were a well-known commercial vehicle manufacturer. They produced a wide range of vehicles from their factory near Glasgow where they also constructed virtually all the necessary components, but Albion also produced a number of commercial vehicles with refuse bodies particularly in the 1940s and 1950s. Several authorities purchased them including Glasgow Corporation and Wycombe Rural District Council. However, despite this interlude into the world of refuse, it was the commercial vehicle market where the company excelled until it was taken over in 1951 by Leyland Motors.

Top: *An Albion 4-ton refuse vehicle which has just been delivered new to Loanhead Town Council, and is being put through its paces by the men. The front opening has its 'greedy board' down for easier loading, but this will be raised as the refuse piles up. Slatted shutters retain the load in transit.* Robert Grieves

BEDFORD

Vauxhall Motors (Bedford's parent company) came into being at the end of the 19th-century via a company called The Vauxhall Iron Works, a producer of marine engines. Moving to Luton in the early 1900s prompted a move into motor car production, but it was not to remain a British firm for long. In the poor economic conditions following World War I, General Motors took over the company in the 1920s as a way of introducing their Chevrolet trucks to the UK market and the Bedford range resulted in 1931. In the years that followed a large number of vehicles were built for the municipal market but only a small percentage were sold as refuse vehicles.

Centre: *As Bedford were not involved crew-cab production and the firm of Reeve-Burgess did many of their conversions. The firm also had a long association with Eagle, as many of the pictures in this book will reveal. Here we see a heavily disguised Bedford with a crew cab and Chelsea body towing a salvage trailer.* Vauxhall Motors Ltd.

BRUSH

This company (better known for trams at the time) manufactured several electric vehicles at its works in Loughborough, which are now famous for diesel and electric locomotive production. However, the firm came first to the local authority market with the supply of vehicles for municipal bus services. Brush had no great impact on the refuse market however, despite some attempts to produce and market tramway dustcarts. These vehicles would have utilised the same infrastructure as the tramway systems, but few civic fathers thought the idea to be practical. However the company did manage to supply six electric 'road' vehicles to the City of Birmingham in 1946/7, but these were not an initial success due to problems with their electrical equipment particularly the Metrovick Drum controllers.

Bottom: *As electric vehicles were simple machines (when compared to petrol vehicles), many firms delved in to this area of production. This was a modified Brush Pony for Fulham.* Arthur Ingram

COMMER/KARRIER.

The well-known Commer marque is closely associated with Karrier, and for many years the Commer-Karrier was a brand in its own right. Commer themselves were actually founded in 1905 as Commercial Cars Ltd., but it was taken over in 1926 by Humber and became part of the Rootes Group in 1928. Meanwhile Karrier Motors Ltd. began life as Clayton & Co. (Huddersfield) and very early in their career, they specialised in several municipal vehicle types, including dustbin wagons. Their main success of course was their light commercial vehicle range, especially a three-wheeled tractor the Cob, which was used extensively by organisations wanting to mechanise their horse-haulage fleets. The firm moved to Luton in 1934 after being taken over by the Rootes group, and part of their old works was used by Harry Ferguson who was working on the Ferguson-Brown tractor, which itself was used by some authorities to tow refuse carts. Just two years after the move from Huddersfield the Karrier 'Bantam' came out in 1936 with a wooden cab. This 4-wheeled vehicle was seen as the successor of the Cob. Whilst Scammell concentrated on the mechanical horse field, with 3- and 6- ton models, Karrier progressed the Bantam. It was very popular with industry and municipal authorities alike, due to its narrow width and excellent manoeuvrability. As well as the normal rigid chassis an articulated tractor unit was also designed, and both types found employment in refuse collection work. Production carried on until 1978, with models being progressively improved, whilst still retaining the light, manoeuvrable concept that had been conceived four decades earlier. Steel cabs were introduced in 1948, and in the late-1950s an electric version of the tractor was introduced proving very useful on municipal work, particularly in London.

Top: *The Commercar refuse vehicle, along with the Karrier Cob, was an important part in the transition period between horse and lorry. This one belongs to Manchester Corporation.* Bob Whewell

Centre: *An example of a Karrier CYR lorry in its 2-ton Low Load Refuse Tipper 'guise of 1929.* Andy Tett

DEARNE

This little known supplier of vehicles began as Reynolds Bros. (Barnsley) Ltd. in 1927. They converted Model 'T' Ford trucks to forward control subsequently calling them Dearne after the river that runs through that part of South Yorkshire. Gaining experience the company then produced their own vehicles from 1928, eventually becoming the Dearne Motor Co. Ltd. Producing 2.5 and 3 ton versions the company suffered the worst of the Depression but the vehicle market had changed during this period and 1935 saw the demise of the operation.

Bottom: *Of similar design to the Karrier seen above, (and also from Yorkshire) this Dearne machine of 1929 looks like something out of a Disney cartoon. No doubt it did the job that it was intended for, but its appointments were very basic; no lights, no starting handle, no horn, no windscreen wipers and only a very basic cab. It probably had a capacity of 1^1/$_2$ tons.* Andy Tett

DENNIS BROTHERS

A pear tree and a bicycle seem unlikely bedfellows as a starting place for a company that went on to become one the UK's largest manufacturers of refuse vehicles. Devon born John Causey Dennis took on an apprenticeship with an ironmonger seeing this as an opportunity to progress in engineering, but it was much to the chagrin of his family. In 1894 he gained an interview with a company called Filmer & Mason Ironmongers in Guildford. He was successful in his career, but he especially flourished after he decided that a bicycle would be useful. Having built one, he decided that instead of using it he would sell it through a local shop. Having made a substantial profit, he made more behind his shop where the frames were suspended from branches of a pear tree, which made assembly easier. His brother Raymond joined him in 1895 but the pear tree inevitably had to go!

In 1899 a milestone was achieved when a De Dion single cylinder engine was fitted to a tricycle, but this venture cost the brothers dearly for the local police fined John the sum of 20 shillings (£1.00) for speeding at 16mph up the Guildford's cobbled High Street!

Even so the tri-cycle enjoyed commercial success, and Dennis's entrepreneurial mind took the next logical step and he duly built a quadri-cycle. This, by the turn of the century, had culminated in a basic motor car. Once again their success was meteoric and with car production underway, they turned their attention to commercial vehicles. By 1904 their first example, a 15cwt van with De Dion 12hp 2-cylinder engine, was on show at Crystal Palace. This van gained further distinction, as it went on to work at the famous Harrods store. From light vans and trucks, buses became an important product line followed by heavy trucks and fire engines, a product with which the 'Dennis' name will always be synonymous. The City of Bradford had the honour of receiving the first Dennis fire engine in 1908, and the company's models are still serving the same city over 90 years later.

Further expansion had taken place in this period and extra manufacturing space was required. To meet this need a Mission Hall in Brixton was acquired in 1908, it was dismantled and transported piece-meal to a new 'green field' site near Guildford.

Left: *A beautifully turned out Dennis Paxit of Redditch Urban District Council, showing the dual purpose design that some local authorities demanded. Dustless loading on the left hand side, with hand-loading for boxes and ordinary bins on the right.* Sheffield City Council

Known as Woodbridge, this site (with continued expansion), was to remain the Dennis factory for 70 years. Throughout World War I, the firm produced thousands of trucks for the war effort, and as early as 1916 their Guildford premises had become one of the largest commercial vehicle manufacturers in Europe. In 1923 nearly 2,000 heavy truck chassis were produced, and although things slowed down to some extent after the Depression, improvements continued to assure Dennis of a sound future. Heavier trucks, pneumatic tyres, improved engines all kept the Company afloat. Local authorities were now slowly becoming mechanised, and by the 1930s Dennis Bros. had successfully ousted the horse from fire services all over Britain; Dennis Lawn Mowers were cutting grass for many municipal authorities.

Looking for the next 'area' to motorise, the Dennis company considered the worsening situation that local authorities found themselves with regard to refuse collection. This was a shrewd move as the population rapidly expanded in the first two decades of the 20th century, and the old horse-drawn dustcarts and cesspit carts had failed to cope with the increasing workload. In 1921 the first Dennis vacuum cesspit emptier was displayed, it met with immediate success and was closely followed by refuse vehicles, street washers and road sweepers. The mould was set for the foreseeable future.

Sales to municipal authorities continued to grow, and included a large range of vehicles, including buses, refuse vehicles, mowers, gully and cesspit emptiers, commercial truck chassis and fire engines. Success on a plate? Not quite, once again the war loomed ahead, and much of the Guildford factory was earmarked for war production. Then, in a cruel blow to the company both John and Raymond Dennis died in 1939. Almost directly (like the Shelvoke factory), the Dennis works went over to military manufacture. This included Churchill tanks and thousands of heavy trucks (just as they had been required to do in World War I). In addition bomb cases and fire-fighting equipment were produced. The few municipal-type vehicles that were constructed were mainly for use on military bases.

After the war mass production resumed with models such as Max, Pax, Horla & Hefty and subsequently the Stork and the Heron, none of which ever made any major impact in the commercial truck industry! So Dennis (once again like S&D) decided to concentrate on what they did best - the specialised vehicle market. Their refuse vehicles became some of the most popular in post-war Britain, particularly the Dennis Paxit with its oscillating packing plate and fibreglass cab. Exports were an important part of the business with many overseas countries purchasing them. The range included sizes from narrow versions (6ft 6ins wide for the narrow back lanes between urban terraces or rural areas), to 24-ton 6 x 4 vehicles.

Above: *One of the most peculiar vehicles ever to come out of the Dennis factory at Guildford, was this weird-looking refuse collector known as the 'Vulture' which was produced for the Borough of Surbiton in Surrey.*

Below: *Another departure from normal convention was the 3-ton Dennis side-loader/tipper. It had been developed from the company's already popular 3-way highway tipper which had sold well into the municipal vehicle market. It offered discharge on either side or at the rear. But whilst this was fine where the ground was stable (say at a highway construction site), but on the rough ground of a rubbish trip it could be quite problematic.*

EAGLE

Eagle Engineering was formed as a limited company by a Mr. R. G. Palmer in 1908, as a manufacturer of petrol engines and farm equipment. They soon progressed to building horse drawn refuse vehicles and road sweepers, and as the municipal market opened up, they began to supply other vehicles to local authorities, including tower lorries for use on tram and trolley bus systems. By 1939 much of their production was earmarked for military application, and during the war the Warwick factory built mobile workshops, barrage balloon vehicles, searchlight trailers and gun platforms. In 1952 Mr. Palmer died and the business was passed on to his son, who immediately introduced a range of new designs with improvements in refuse collection vehicles, gully and cesspit emptiers, and mobile television masts. In the mid-1960s the firm was bought out by Hanger Motors of Birmingham but after just 30 months they sold it on to Combat Engineering. This firm did no better, and inside 12-months it had been sold on to the engineering firm Hestair. Under the name Hestair Eagle, the firm became very successful, and they manufactured a wide range of vehicles, including fire appliances, road sweepers, road tankers and, of course, refuse collection vehicles. Today the name of Eagle is still extant, but now intimately associated with Dennis.

Eagle were a very inspired company who were not only forward-thinking and but were also relatively inexpensive, a fact that endeared them to many cash-strapped local councils. Their range was therefore to be seen in service over a wide area, and the very successful Compressload and Compressmore models were to be found all over the country in the 1960s. Yet it had not always been the case, and prior to 1952 many strange creations had emerged from the Warwick plant; rotating bodies; round side-loading bodies; and front loaders with ejection discharge.

Top: *One of the innovative ideas that came out of the Eagle factory was this ingenious Speedyload model. Similar in principle to the Laird Shark, refuse was tipped into a rear hopper where a rotating drum pulverised it. It was then directed to the front of the body by strakes. This 1961 view shows a Speedyload body fitted on to a Bedford TK chassis, and is seen just before entering service with the Borough of Bermondsey Engineer and Surveyor's Department.* Vauxhall Motors Ltd.

Centre: *This picture shows another Bedford-Eagle combination prior to delivery to Wokingham RDC. This time we see a Bedford A5 type chassis fitted with a Compressmore body, which was both an inexpensive and very popular machine.* Vauxhall Motors Ltd.

Bottom: *This shows a potentially effective type of refuse collection system which is formed from articulated Newcastle-type refuse trailers and Bedford TK tractor units. This system had been developed from the mechanical horse concept, in which one trailer unit could be filled or emptied whilst another was being taken to its destination.* Vauxhall Motors Ltd.

EDISON - (ELECTRICARS).

Edison Accumulators Ltd. are well known as electric vehicle suppliers in a number of countries, particularly Great Britain and the USA. However much of the time, if not all, they only supplied the electrical equipment and batteries. Their marketing department obviously did a wonderful job in maintaining the company's name on vehicles despite the fact that bodies and chassis were invariably built by others. GMC chassis were often utilised as were Walker and Lansden. Bodies varied according to local builders' facilities. In 1920 Edison sold its UK vehicle operation to the Electricar Company based initially in Landor Street, Birmingham. Production later moved to Lawley Street, but ten years on found them at Webb Lane, Hall Green, again in Birmingham. Amalgamations were in the air by 1939 as the company merged with Morrison & Sons Ltd. becoming Associated Electric Vehicle Manufacturers Ltd. (A.E.V.M). Morrisons had concentrated their range of vehicles on the lighter end of the market whereas Electricars had the heavier duty products. Although the two product lines were complimentary, rationalisation soon followed. The Hall Green operation was closed in 1944, the A.E.V.M. enterprise ended and Morrisons continued production of new ranges of vehicles from their Leicester factory under the name Morrison-Electricar Ltd. producing refuse vehicles up to 14 cu yds capacity.

Top: *An Electricar-Shefflex combination with a Fore & Aft tipper supplied to Sheffield in the 1930s.* Sheffield City Council
Centre: *The fact that Electricar was a local firm undoubtedly influenced Birmingham Salvage Department when they placed their orders for new vehicles. For example Birmingham bought 25 Electricars in 1920 alone, with the idea of displacing horse-drawn carts. This Electricar was supplied to Birmingham in 1938 and lasted until the mid-60s, but it was later restored at the city's Museum of Science & Industry.* Roger F De Boer

FODEN/ERF

The well known company of Foden from Sandbach in Cheshire had already been active in the refuse collection vehicle market since the days of steam when their overtype wagon was used in this work. In due course the company adopted the internal combustion engine, but it literally split into two when Mr. E. R. Foden decided to break away from his firm, he rented one of Jennings workshops to produce his own chassis, the ERF. The chassis came complete with a Jennings cab, and this was to set the scene for a successful relationship for many years where the majority of ERF chassis were built with Jennings cabs. In 1963 the company took over the assets of Jennings, but in 1971 the two Jennings brothers decided to leave and set up their own operation as Jennings Coachwork Ltd., in Crewe until 1993 when they sold the company and retired.
Bottom: *This FG6 8x4 chassis, with a Gardner 6LW engine was fitted with a GWL 40cu yard body and used by Sheffield to transfer waste from the city to landfill sites in the surrounding countryside which often involved substantial journeys.* Sheffield City Council

FORD

The first model 'T' Ford trucks arrived in this country from America in 1908, and UK production commenced at Trafford Park Works in 1911 before moving to Dagenham in 1931. Ford trucks appeared as refuse vehicles for many years but the 'D' series (introduced in 1965) made the most impact. Like Bedford however they were into mass production of standard types and not able to incorporate all the specialist requirements of municipal vehicles. Thus chassis were again farmed out for cab conversions, and chassis alterations.

Top: *The popularity of Ford's new D series chassis in highway and general council work soon helped the company break in to the refuse collection market as local authorities began to standardise their vehicle fleets. However, Ford still had to rely heavily on outside bodybuilders for chassis flitching and the fitment of a PTO for the specialist refuse vehicle market.* Sheffield City Council

GARNER

This Tyseley firm had an interesting history going back to Henry Garner who began selling cars in 1907. Various moves saw him develop his company as Henry Garner Ltd. A somewhat spurious beginning saw the 'Garner' name appear on commercial lorries, following a mysterious order for 200 vehicles for South America. The company branched out in to all sorts of vehicles including their special 'Busvan', tractors and small-wheeled low-loading petrol engined refuse vehicles. In 1933 Sentinel took over and production moved to Shrewsbury, and this resulted in a new more conventional cab design with a resemblance to the Sentinel 'S' range cab. The move may have hidden various financial problems within the company, which was soon liquidated. However the name survived and in 1936 Garner Motors Ltd. began production at a factory in Acton after the name was revived by a group of ex-Chrysler businessmen.

Centre: *A Garner AE model supplied to Hackney Borough Council in the spring of 1929.*

GARRETT.

The firm of Richard Garrett & Sons of Leiston in Suffolk were one of the pioneers in this field. Following the death of a certain William Cracey, Richard Garrett purchased his forge in Leiston in 1783. Engineering in the form of threshing drums and other farm machinery soon began and an example of their portable engine was shown in the Great Exhibition at Crystal Palace in 1851. Orders flowed in, traction engines were developed and in the early years of the 20th-century the first 'Overtype' wagons rolled off the line, of which a few found their way into local authority work. In 1917 Garrett's produced their first electric vehicles.

Bottom: *The year 1922 saw the first Garrett 'Undertype' steam wagon emerge and it undoubtedly impressed several councils. This one was supplied to Haslemere UDC and it was quite versatile, for after swapping bodies it could double as a highways vehicle, cesspit emptier or gully emptier.* Suffolk Record Office

Top: *It was the Garrett electric vehicle, that really offered so much potential, and here we see one of the main types produced with Tudor Accumulator equipment. The baskets used as skeps were known here as creels, a term taken from the fishing industry.* Robert Grieves.

Centre: *One particular Garrett caught the imagination of Glasgow Corporation who had a major crisis with their refuse collection service south of the Clyde. Therefore, recycling of refuse was mooted and a huge plant was built at Craigton Road in Govan for this purpose. Due to the peculiarity of the tenement buildings around Glasgow a considerable amount of refuse was collected at night. Electric vehicles were ideal because they were quiet and would fit in with the plant and other criteria, which required a very specific design of vehicle. Following reluctance by other manufacturers to come up with anything suitable, Garrett's spent an enormous amount of time and effort to produce the vehicle that became known as the GTZ. A forward mounted cab preceded a very low loading line body on a specially designed chassis. It also had side tipping, a tight turning circle and 'Tudor' Battery power to give a minimum of 40 miles per charge. One interesting aspect of the design came about because space and weight on the chassis was at a premium due to the special design and mass of batteries. In theory, the vehicles would only ever tip at one location (i.e. Govan) it therefore raised the question, why fit every unit with a tipping gear? Obviously to do so would further reduce the payload, increase costs and maintenance, so why not fit the gear into the structure of the plant? This was in fact done. The prototype was completed on 25th February 1927, tested around Leiston and then packed off by rail to Glasgow. Eventually a total of 54 GTZ units were delivered to Glasgow on solid tyres. A smaller batch was later sent on pneumatic tyres. Neighbouring Paisley also tried a couple, but apart from that no other councils took up this particular design. One other variation, a solitary diesel-engined version was also tried. The GTZ system was finally phased out of Glasgow in 1964, but it had given 37 years of service to the city.* Suffolk Record Office

WM. GLOVER & SONS LTD

This firm, based in Warwick, dated back to the early days of refuse collection, when they built a wide range of specialised horse drawn wagons to tempt would be purchasers. Their 'Champion' Dust Van featured screw tipping gear, patent axles, sliding covers, wind-guards and driver's seat! It was awarded the 'London County Council Premium for Best Van' out of over 300 designs. The sliding 'Chelsea' type lids were built in a frame that could be removed from the cart leaving an open sided wagon. In addition the rear section could be rolled forward on brass rollers clear of the back to give better discharge when tipping. Various mergers and take-overs ensued until the well-known firm of Glover, Webb & Liversidge was formed.

Bottom: *Taken from the Glover catalogue, this illustration shows the company's 'Champion' Dust Van which came in capacities from 2cu yards to 4cu yards and had screw tipping gear.*

Above: *This Glover, Webb, Liversidge body, with the screw feed clearly visible in the vehicle's rear hopper, was known as the Musketeer. Fitted on the Karrier chassis the two went together like strawberries and cream. It was a very successful and inexpensive machine, and when it came to council tendering time it was often competing directly with the Norba screw-feed RCV. This example from 1970 was in service with Manchester Corporation.*

Below: *On the 23rd June 1993 this Karrier Bantam with a GWL body was released from duty with the Royal Household and sent to Sunderland on the back of a low-loader. Most Refuse vehicles had the owning authority's name sign-written on the cab door such as APPLEBY in WESTMORLAND RURAL DISTRICT COUNCIL etc. However, GGX 232N in its green livery was inscribed slightly differently as: CROWN ESTATE PAVING COMMISSION, THE LODGE, PARK SQUARE WEST, REGENTS PARK and adorned*

GLOVER WEBB & LIVERSIDGE

This firm was closely associated with Commer and many of their bodies were fitted to Commer or Karrier chassis, but other manufacturers would be considered if the customer so wished. They built a great many side loaders (as did most other manufacturers), but they also made a 'Dual Tip' body (a fore & aft tipper) and a packing plate system. However, they were probably best known for their 'Musketeer' body, which featured a screw feed to pulverise the refuse on entry to the body. The company struggled for a long time in the 1960s but came through difficult times to eventually prove successful. They also had at least one prestigious customer for they held the warrant 'By Royal Appointment to HM Queen Elizabeth'!

Buckingham Palace, as with any other 'house', produced refuse which in turn had to be collected and disposed of. For many years this was done with a Karrier 'Bantam' chassis fitted with a GWL side loader body. The vehicle covered the Royal Estate around Chelsea Barracks, the Palace and a part of Regents Park. Side-loaders had done this work at the palace for many years. In 1975 the old vehicle was replaced by a Karrier 'Bantam' registered GGX 232N. Although later than the period covered by this book, this vehicle (with its standard chassis, 122" wheelbase and Perkins 4203 diesel engine) has an interesting story surrounding its eventual preservation in Sunderland. This preservation came about in a strange way, which all began one weekend in September 1990.

The Hogarth family - staunch Karrier Bantam enthusiasts and Sunderland football supporters - came down to London from Wearside and stayed in a hotel near Piccadilly. A gentle amble down Pall Mall found them staring at the above vehicle in a park. On inquiring the driver advised them that the Queen owned it and it was for sale so, if they were interested they should ring Buckingham Palace to find out the price. Back home, from 9.15 on Monday morning the Hogarth's made call after call in an attempt to contact Buckingham Palace. However, at 11.30am a knock on the front door revealed the local police! Due to the high security measures following several London bombing incidents, British Telecom had contacted the local constabulary to find out why so many calls were emanating from this particular number for the Royal Household.

After showing the police the video film of the vehicle, some Dinky toys and their other Karrier Bantams that were being restored, the officers gave the Hogarths permission for the contact to proceed. Eventually the right person was found, but the first response was that the vehicle was not available. Undaunted, when the photos of the day came back they were despatched to the Palace, six weeks later, a price had been offered and accepted. However they couldn't have the vehicle immediately, as it was still working but were advised to ring back periodically to check when it would become redundant. On Saturday 9th May 1993 Sunderland played Liverpool in the FA Cup Final at Wembley; our intrepid Sunderland supporters were there of course. Prior to the trip they telephoned the Queen's Secretary to make the final arrangements for the acquisition and subsequently the lorry was duly preserved.

GUY MOTORS LTD.

Again this is another manufacturer who will normally be best remembered for their heavy trucks and buses, although they also built a smaller range of commercial chassis which, from time to time, found their way into the refuse vehicle market. The company was founded in 1914 at Fallings Park just outside Wolverhampton, but due to the hostilities of the time the factory was soon producing various armaments for the war effort. A few chassis were also built, and this was followed by car production until 1924 when the company decided to concentrate on commercials. In 1923 their first 2½ - 3-ton battery-electric refuse vehicle chassis was produced on solid tyres and using Exide-Ironclad batteries it had a maximum speed of 10 mph over a 45 mile range. Only very few were ever produced, but Guy also built the bodies with hand tipping and an option on electrical operation. The petrol engined version appeared in 1924 equipped with hydraulic tipping, and a choice of pneumatic tyres from 1927 onwards. Specialist refuse vehicle production appears to have ceased in 1930, but after this date some bodies were manufactured for Guy at the Pilot Works in Bolton (which subsequently became Edbro). After over 25 years of successful operation the company collapsed, and its assets transferred to Guy Motors (Europe) Ltd. which was bought by Jaguar in 1961. A few years later Jaguar was acquired by BMC and thus Guy became a division of the British Leyland Motor Corporation.

Above: *A heavily touched up photograph used by Guy's publicity department shows a Vixen chassis with a Derby body, which was delivered to Bromsgrove UDC in 1935.* Ron Lucas

Centre: *A Guy chassis with an all-steel side loader body from Pilot, which was supplied to Carmarthern RDC in 1943. Being a wartime vehicle, the RCV shows a number of special features; cowled headlights, white flashes on the rear mudguard, and above all no spare tyre. Due to rubber shortages only a wheel rim was supplied, and operators had to try and find an old tyre to fit.* Ron Lucas

HALLEY,

Another Glasgow based manufacturer, this time at Yoker, who also had another factory in Newcastle for some time. Halley produced a wide range of petrol engined chassis from 30 cwt to 6 tons, and they survived until 1935. One of their advertising slogans was 'The Height Of Efficiency!' This referred to their W21 model with a 10 cu yd side loading body, hauling a 7 cu yd trailer. The body was equipped with Bromilow & Edwards twin under-floor Hydraulic tipping rams, whilst the trailer had hand power tipping only. The company was able to offer their customers a choice of doors on the side-loader; spring actuated dustless doors; circular sliding doors; canvas covers or flat spring loaded!

Bottom: *This is the the vehicle referred to in the text, and the picture shows a wonderful array of wheel sizes and types on one model. This particular unit was supplied to Deptford Borough Council in 1931.* Jim Wilkinson - Halley Archives

JENNINGS

The body builders J. H. Jennings & Sons Ltd. is interesting due to their longevity in the vehicle business. George Jennings founded the company in 1764 as wheelwrights and blacksmiths in the tiny village of Little Warford in Cheshire. A successful enterprise, it was passed down from father to son until John Henry Jennings decided he wanted to do his own thing and split away from the main family stream, setting up his own business in 1897 in nearby Mottram-St-Andrew, eventually moving to Sandbach in 1902. His son, Frank joined the business in 1915 at the highly inflated wage of 3d (approx. 1.25p) per week! In 1917 the company expanded to Crewe Road in Sandbach, by this time all types of specialised bodywork were being produced. including horseboxes, mobile libraries, cattle trucks and of course refuse bodies. (see also Foden/ERF)

Top: *A Jennings side-loader on a Bedford O Type chassis. with a salvage crate on the roof. Wonderfully sign-written, this vehicle went to Sandbach Urban District Council.* Chris Taylor

LAIRD

Laird (of Anglesey) began life on another British island in 1940. The company commenced operations as Saunders Roe, erecting Catalina flying boats on the Isle of Wight, and specialised in aluminium welding techniques. In addition to the flying boats, they made bus bodies, Bailey Bridges, military vehicles and Trackway (the aluminum roadway that could be laid out on rough ground from a roll). Many other associated products came out of the factory, including refuse vehicles that had aluminium outer body casing.The threat of invasion and the formation of a restricted military area on the Isle Of Wight saw the company moving to the quietude of Anglesey. Another factor was found in the quiet anchorage for flying boats that were being returned for overhaul.

Laird, as the company eventually became, began producing the Shark refuse collection vehicle body, which in effect was a large rotating drum similar to a standard front loading washing machine. The license to produce this coming from Kuka in Germany in the 1960s, the continually rotating drum was noisy when empty but became quieter as the load increased. However, it had a good compaction rate with strakes inside the drum which funnelled the rubbish forward. The rotating discharge system, ideally suited for a transfer station or pit, could be quite a lengthy procedure on a flat surface as it entailed reversing the drum so the refuse gradually wound itself back out again. The firm are still engaged in refuse vehicle production today, and currently produce the successful Faun intermittent loader.

Centre: *During the 1970s the Leyland Boxer chassis proved to be popular with municipalities, this demonstrator is equipped with the well-matched Gilbraith crew cab and the Shark rotary body.*
Left: *Illustrating the next generation of both body and chassis, this Leyland Constructor is mounted with the Laird Rotopress body, of which over 33,500 have been built world-wide.* Faun (Anglesey).

LEYLAND

This famous manufacturer began with steam waggons in 1896, with internal combustion appearing in 1904. Leyland became a vast empire taking in many manufacturers including AEC (Thornycroft, & Maudslay), Albion and Scammell. The company also joined Daimler, Guy, Morris and Austin when it merged with British Motor Holdings in 1968 to become British Leyland. The Super Comet and the later Boxer range of chassis were utilised considerably for refuse work but fell into the same category as Ford and Bedford if anything special was required to the chassis. Many of the Leyland crew-cab conversions were carried out by Gilbraith Commercials of Chorley.

Top: *One of the early Leyland productions, which features a three-way tipper built for the Westminster Wharfage Co. at Vauxhall. These vehicles were easy to load by virtue of the fact that the body sides were hinged longitudinally and could be folded down.* Andy Tett

NORBA

The other Screw Feed design, was closely associated with Dennis chassis originally, although this was to change as the years went by. Norba bodies were imported in the early 1960s, from Kalmar in Sweden where production began. Later they were assembled in Letchworth, only a stone's throw from S&D! Their original tipping bodies were of steel and designed to flex as the load increased. Indeed with the conical shaped screw compacting to a tremendous extent (compared to other designs at the time), the body could often be seen to be swelling under the load! Size for size the Norba would frequently carry far more tonnage than its contemporaries could. The drive to the early screw feed units was mechanical with a dog-tooth gear at the join between body and hopper, which would disengage when tipping. If the screw jammed or stopped due to being fully loaded a 'shear-pin' would snap to ensure no damage was done to the mechanism. The driver carried a bag of pins with him as replacements each time this happened. Later models were hydraulically driven with blow-off valves fitted. Eventually production became totally UK-based, the company however were always controlled financially from overseas. The Demountable, Roll on - Roll off vehicle builder Multilift in Shrewsbury was part of the Finnish Multilift Company and incorporated into a huge organisation called Partek. When this firm encapsulated the Swedish Norba production, it had a far reaching effect on the UK based operation and led to the closure of both the Letchworth, and Hitchin factories. Afterwards, and with all production moved to Shrewsbury, Norba went from strength to strength to become the leading supplier of refuse trucks in the UK.

Centre: *A 1967 Dennis Pax with a Norba screw feed packing system. Local authorities took a lot of convincing to change to this type of compaction as it was completely different from anything seen before, but after a successful demonstration authorities like Stoke-on-Trent, Colchester, Slough and Glasgow had major fleets.* Bill Aldridge

Bottom: *A Norba body and a Reeve-Burgess crew cab feature on this Karrier chassis supplied to the Borough of Bedford.* Cargotec

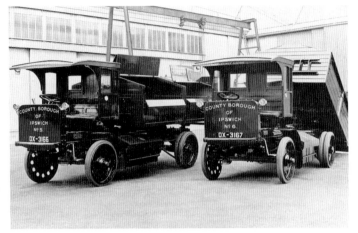

RANSOMES

This Ipswich firm are well known for their farming implements, traction engines and travelling cranes. Less known is the fact that they also produced electric refuse vehicles from 1915 onwards. These were very crude with wooden open cabs, but some were given delightful and impracticable retractable canvas 'umbrellas' for cover. They were also augmented with hand tipping gear. Wooden spoked wheels with solid Dunlop tyres were fitted at first but these soon gave way to very distinctive metal wheel centres. They were powered by Ironclad-Exide Batteries rated at 5.5hp with a chain-driven rear axle, but along with other vehicles of this type a speed limit of 12mph was imposed.

Top: *Birmingham Corporation are thought to have bought the first two Ransomes electric vehicles in 1915, (with 5 more in 1923), and Sheffield came shortly afterwards. Other authorities included Cardiff, Motherwell, Newport, Rotherham, Willesden, Worthing, Warrington and the County Borough Ipswich (as seen here in 1922). Some models were also exported to such places as Penang (Malaya) and Hobart (Tasmania).* Rural History Centre Reading University

SCAMMELL

George Scammell began exercising his engineering skills in the late 19th-century from a works in Fashion Street, Spitalfields, London, near Liverpool St. Station. With steady progression and innovative ideas the Company survived World War I, expanded and moved to the famous Tolpits Lane site at Watford. Their innovations gained them a great reputation for specialist vehicles, which was enjoyed throughout their existence. The huge tractor units with imposing names such as the 'Pioneer', 'Explorer', 'Constructor', 'Contractor', 'Commander' and so on are well known.

But Scammell also looked at the other end of the market and in a fit of wonderful logic and simplicity produced the 'Mechanical Horse'. It amazed all those who saw it at its launch in 1933. A three wheeled lorry with a 2.09 litre side valve petrol engine and gearbox behind the cab. It was devised for in-town suburban work, usually hauling a short articulated trailer with incredible manoeuvrability. It was an immediate success particularly with the railway companies, and this story is well told in the NOSTALGIA ROAD books dealing with railway-owned road vehicles. Both the military and the utilities realised its advantages, not only by swapping trailers but also through the fact that it could go almost everywhere, especially the places that horse-drawn vehicles had previously served. The Scammell Scarab was introduced in 1948, and over 20,000 were eventually constructed some as rigid trucks for particular uses including refuse collection.

Centre: *One of the most manoeuvrable RCVs ever, this 3-wheel 3-ton Scammell Mechanical Horse with a side-loading body was bought by Leeds City Council's Cleansing Department in 1938 for collecting refuse from the local markets.* H S Transport Collection.

Bottom: *A more conventional Mechanical Horse, this time fitted with a low loading Alex Laurie body and a slogan from the Royal Burgh Of Ayr that states 'We Require Public Assistance - Help Us Keep The Town Clean'.* Robert Grieves

SEDDON

Seddon or rather Foster & Seddon were quite late entering the commercial vehicle market when their first truck appeared in 1937. Few were produced for municipal work until, having gone through several changes, the firm of Seddon Atkinson began producing a purpose-built crew-cab chassis in the 1970s which was specifically aimed at the municipal market. Apart from S&D and Dennis no other maker did this and 'commercial' chassis had to be driven to a 'crew-cab builder' before further delivery to the body builders. The result was not only time consuming but also often a compromise and not a very elegant one at that! A useful association was the Edbro works in Bolton, who bodied a great many Seddon vehicles.

Top: *A Seddon RCV with a Perkins Diesel and a Laird Shark body, which was No. 54 in the Manchester fleet. The unusual shaped body held a rotating drum which pulverised the refuse.*

SENTINEL of Shrewsbury

As mentioned earlier none of the steam engine builders were very successful in the municipal field, but Sentinel did make some valiant efforts. The first Sentinels originated from Alley & McClellan Ltd., of Polmadie, Glasgow in 1906, but in 1915 production was transferred to Shrewsbury where they were still producing steam lorries for export in 1949. Sentinel was eventually taken over by Rolls Royce Engines, whilst Transport Vehicles (Warrington) Ltd. continued a limited production from spares Sentinel left behind.

Centre: *A Skoda dustbin wagon? Yes, there was such a beast and Skoda built over 400 dustbin wagons for Sentinel between 1925 and 1927, of which 6 were fitted out as Ash Can carriers. The low-level body must have been quite a design achievement in view of the underfloor engine. In this system full bins are obviously taken to the tip, and empty ones left in their stead; more information on this system would be appreciated.* Anthony Thomas

SHEFFLEX

Shefflex was founded by John Sherwood, and despite claims to the contrary, this firm could justifiably state they produced the first 'fore & aft' tipper. It was a horse drawn two-wheel cart; with wooden wheels of 6ft diameter! After loading a few bins the 'driver' would hand-wind the body forward to shift the refuse to the front. In 1946 they patented a new dustless loading system which was first exhibited at the 1947 Blackpool Public Cleansing Exhibition; the system initially used a special bin designed for the purpose. Their more conventional Fore & Aft vehicle came along (more often than not on a Dennis 'PAX' chassis) and this was operated with two under-floor hydraulic rams.

Bottom: *Shefflex vehicles were built at Rutland Street in Sheffield and therefore a local builder was politically attractive to the authority . Sheffield became the largest user of Shefflex refuse vehicles but other councils such as Rotherham, Colne Valley and a few others also dabbled. Here a Shefflex "Hygienic' dustless body is fitted on an Electricar chassis.* Sheffield City Council

Shelvoke & Drewry, were arguably the best-known name in the refuse collection business. Harry Shelvoke came from Melverley in Shropshire, and moved from Wolseley to Lacre in 1911. Here he took up the position of General Manager, at which point he met their Chief Engineer Drewry, who had risen to fame with his petrol-driven railcar. Together the two worked privately on producing a much-needed small truck that would be both cheap to run and highly manoeuvrable With its transverse engine, their new design was produced in a barn using a lot of Lacre components. Once the truck was proven and, more importantly a market need established, they left to start their own business.

Above: *After building a new 6,600 square foot factory on a 'green-field site' in Letchworth, the S&D Freighter was born. Starting with 30 employees rapid expansion ensued, and by the end of 1924 (just over two years since its inception) the 100th Freighter emerged. By November 1929 the 1,000th unit rolled out of the factory which had seen further expansion and was working double shifts. By 1932 the company had grown to 350 employees working in 40,500 square feet of space. The Freighter was ostensibly a commercial chassis, but its conversion to refuse collection work was easily achieved. The above picture shows a beautifully restored Freighter of 1922 vintage. Sheffield City Council.*

Early orders came from the municipalities of Deptford and Wallasey, and from these small beginnings S&D progressed to cover the whole country. The Freighter was a simple vehicle, and it's unique design can be more fully appreciated when one realised it contained some 200 less components than a conventional lorry of the day! Right from the inception of the refuse vehicle variation, tipping was by powered hydraulics and these compared well with S&D's competitors which were still largely hand screw operated. Pneumatic tyres came along of course as did a steering wheel and covered cab (still with open sides though). Accordingly, many attempted to emulate the Freighter with reduced height floors, small wheels and narrow width, but no-one could stop the runaway success of this little truck. Not only did it sweep the country in its refuse vehicle guise, but it also found fame as a commercial truck.

Although the S&D Freighter was progressively modernised; with electric lighting; full cab; higher payload and so on, it began to lose favour in the commercial market which by the 1930s was expanding rapidly into larger vehicles with higher speeds and better payloads. It was clearly evident that S&D were becoming so popular in the local authority market that they concentrated in that area from then on. Development progressed of course as the Freighter gave way to more and more modern designs. In 1937 the 'E type' emerged, aesthetically this was an amazingly different machine, but underneath its pedigree was plainly obvious. Whilst Perkins Diesel engines were introduced that year, S&D stuck rigidly to their 'Petrol Engine' and still gave a 10-year guarantee with every vehicle! The Freighter continued in production until 1948 alongside the 'E Type'.

During World War II few refuse vehicles were produced as S&D, were heavily engaged in war work, and their most famous contract was for 4-man submarines! After the war, the 'W Type' appeared from the factory in 1946, to the designs of Charles K. Edwards who had previous experience with Morris-Commercial and Guy.

Hand in hand with refuse collection was the matter of street cleansing and gully-emptying. Here again S&D produced a specific vehicle, which led to a strong market position both at home and abroad. So successful was this new truck that 3,200 were produced up to 1961 by which time of course it too was being superseded by later developments.

Edwards retired in 1955, and was eventually replaced by Tom Tillson, who had previously been with both Dennis and Daimler. It was Tillson who designed the next, and very successful range the 'T Type' which brought S&D into the modern world. The S&D petrol engine had by now given way to the all-conquering diesel engine, with 4 & 6 cylinder versions being used. These were mainly from Perkins of course but Leyland engines were an option on some heavier chassis. The wooden cabs waned in favour of fibreglass, which were produced at Letchworth, and the 'T Type' with its distinctively designed cab soon became commonplace throughout the world. Shelvoke & Drewry continued to dominate the refuse vehicle market throughout the period of this book and well after until the firm's demise in the 1980s.

Above: *The 'W Type' ('W' standing for steering wheel) swept away many of the archaic facets of the Freighter that had been perpetuated in the 'E Type'. Gone was the transverse-mounted engine, and with it the side-mounted radiator, from now on the already famous S&D roundel would be displayed proudly in the centre of a forward located radiator. The gearbox was also now of conventional style with a gear-stick in lieu of the original tiller.*

Below: *This view shows one of the well-liked TN models in service with Scunthorpe Cleansing Department. A significant reason for the design of the T series was to take advantage of the increasing axle and vehicle loading limits, which had now reached 14-tons on two axles. This led to the range of TN, TW, TX, TZ models and eventually the TY when the 16-ton two-axle vehicle was introduced. The 'T' range and Pakamatic served Shelvoke & Drewry well throughout the 1960s until the 1970s when the 'Revopak' entered the market.* H S Transport Collection

TILLING-STEVENS

Based at the Victoria Works, Maidstone, Tillings were another electric vehicle manufacturer from the early years of this century utilising Exide Ironclad Batteries. They also manufactured petrol and petrol-electric units. Based on the Karrier Cob, they planned to produce a three-wheel 'Mechanical Horse' with an 18ft turning circle. Capacity was 2-3 tons, and a similar four-wheel version was also available. It is thought that only three were ever built, and none were sold. Tilling-Stevens also disappeared when they were taken over by the Rootes Group (in 1953) who were then manufacturing Commer and Karrier vehicles.

Top: *This Tilling Stevens 3-wheel electric tractor featured automatic coupling with the trailer. They were said to be ideal for street market cleansing, where stand trailers could be left for refuse dumping and then picked up at the end of the day.*

TRANSPORT EQUIPMENT (THORNYCROFT) LTD.

Based for many years in Basingstoke, this firm commenced business at Church Wharf, Chiswick in 1864 as the Steam Carriage & Waggon Co. John Isaac Thornycroft was the inspiration for the company, having been originally involved in producing steam launches; these led to a small steam waggon in 1896. Very soon petrol engines were introduced and the company went from strength to strength until the 1960s when they were taken over by AEC. They used various manufacturers' bodies including Eagle.

Centre: *With horse-drawn carts standing in the rear, this picture shows the 'new era' of refuse collection in the City Of Westminster. Built in 1899, as works number 11, this Thornycroft steamer must have been under some form of evaluation when this picture was taken, as it has a banner proclaiming that it has run 69,000 miles. Imagine driving that distance on wheels with wooden spokes and solid tyres along cobbled streets!* Arthur Ingram

VULCAN

This firm began producing vehicles in 1902 from their Southport factory, a small number entered council work, but they were more inclined towards general haulage. The Great Western Railway were a customer (see the Nostalgia Road book on this subject). In 1938 Vulcan were taken over by Tilling Stevens, but the name was not dropped until 1952/3 at the time of the Rootes takeover (see above).

Bottom: *Supposedly taken in 1931, this picture shows a new Vulcan as it poses with the maker's ornate figurine (a mythical god) on top of the exposed radiator. Number 10 in the Rochdale Corporation Cleansing Department fleet, it has the registered number DK 6723. Other little features are the centrally located 'bulb' horn protruding through the cab just below the windscreen and the acetylene lights. The Corporation obviously believed in advertising in order to keep the volume of rubbish to a minimum.* Andy Tett

WALKER BROS. - PAGEFIELD

Above: *This is not a furniture van, but a Walker-NCB refuse vehicle with a moving floor system based on the Pagefield Paragon chassis converted to electric traction.* Sheffield City Council

Walker Brothers tends to be a 'forgotten' manufacturer, but it is one with an excellent pedigree. Started by John Scarisbrook Walker in 1866, at a tiny premises in Queen Street, Wigan, this firm began producing items of engineering for the local (and not so local) mining industry. In 1869 Walker was joined by his brother Thomas and together they went on to make larger items of mining machinery, industrial fans, air compressors and so on.

Expansion meant moving; in 1873 a green field site called Page's Fields was selected for a new factory which became known as Pagefield Ironworks. In the late 1880s steam locomotive production commenced, a total of 114 locomotives were eventually built there. Then came road vehicles and 1904 saw the first motor car; and commercial vehicle production began in 1908, these included Char-a-Bancs, box-vans and tippers. Like most manufacturers of their day they produced almost everything on site.

The tipper vehicles inevitably caught the eye of the local authorities and in 1922 Southport Urban District Council approached Walker Bros. to replace their horse-drawn fleet of refuse collection vehicles. This resulted in what became the 'Pagefield System'. A 5-ton 'W' type tipper chassis was mounted with a sub-frame that could carry a demountable body.

The body carried on tiny solid tyres (on 20 inch wheels) to give a low loading height, was horse-drawn around the collecting area. When full a lorry would come along demount an empty body and then winch on the full one to take to the tip. The action was achieved by using drive shafts off the top of the gearbox across the chassis and up the sub-frame through skew gears to the winch. Many authorities used this system, Liverpool for instance at one stage had over 50 vehicles servicing some 200 horse-drawn containers.

The Drinkwater Company operated the system in some London boroughs, and this was possibly the first instance of privatisation with demountable bodies! Walkers also produced a few electric vehicles in the 1920s. However the usual improvements added to the benefits of the internal combustion engined Pagefield System over the years and then in 1932 the 'Prodigy' was introduced - a fixed body unit with side or rear loading, small wheels powered by the Wolverhampton based 'Meadows' 4ELV petrol engine. Yet the cab design was amazingly similar to the contemporary S&D unit!

Above: *The Pagefield 'Paladin' vehicle may have disappeared into obscurity but the word became synonymous with the large containers that were fitted with wheels and were known the world over as 'Paladin Bins'. The Paladin license was taken on by Eagle, and thus it survived as a system down to the 'wheelie bin' era. This picture shows a Paladin operation in the Islington Borough Council area, and to the rear of this petrol-engined model a loader can be seen with one of the pump-truck trolleys used to move the huge bins between property and collection vehicle.*

Below: *This view shows the third type of engine fitted to the Walker-Pagefield, as this model in service with the City of Birmingham boasts a Perkins diesel engine. Here No. 122 extols the virtue of recycling paper, as it continues on its round. Discharge on these vehicles was achieved by reversing the action of the scuppers to the rear of the body. Both pictures Arthur Ingram.*

In 1934 the Pagefield became the first vehicle fitted with the Perkins Oil Engine. Following on from this, the letter 'P' seemed to dictate the models names and following Prodigy we had Paragon, Pegasus, Pompian, Paladin, Pegasix, Plantagenet and Pathfinder. The 'Paragon' Refuse Vehicle appeared in the 1930s looking more like a removal lorry than a dustcart. It carried a 5-ton load, some were fitted with moving floors, an electrical winch was tried on others to lift the bins up for discharge, and another idea was a mobile frame running on guides high up on the body sides that again carried the bin. Inside the body were four semi-circular sections or plates known as 'scuppers' that worked on a telescopic principal and were operated by chains from a power drive from the engine via the gearbox. To start loading the scuppers were all located to the rear of the body, but as loading progressed each in turn moved forwards simultaneously shifting the refuse and compacting it.

During the 1930s many towns were beginning to build low-rise flats and tenements to meet the housing needs of the era, and with their narrow flights of stairs and landings a new solution to refuse collection had to be devised. The answer was to be found with communal chutes, below which a large refuse container could be placed. However, because these bins were so large, it was impossible to load them into the conventional RCV and the entire container would (at first) be exchanged for an empty one, with the full one being taken on a vehicle to the tip.

Densmore Walker, who had been a director since 1923, realised the benefits of devising equipment to empty the bin into the RCV. Whether the vehicle tackle or the Paladin came first is a moot point, but Walker devised a tall circular bin with small wheels. This bin could be lifted at the rear of the collection vehicle by winch driven cable gear, and then tipped into the body. Although the general adoption of this system did not come until the end of World War II, it proved totally successful. It continued in wide-spread use through to the introduction of hydraulics on RCVs, and will undoubtedly still be around in the new millennium.

After the war existing lines of RCV's, Mobile Cranes, Industrial Fans, and Rail Cars were still in production but a new line in converting petrol cars to diesel was also started. To this end a new company was formed in 1948, Walkers & County Cars Ltd. Becoming County Commercial Cars, they produced the Jetka Municipal body.

The last Pagefield system was fitted to an Albion chassis in the mid-1950s and supplied to Stafford UDC. A number of Paragon chassis were supplied to Northern Coachbuilders who converted them into 10 ton GVW electric refuse collectors, they were known as Walker NCB's and from this move came the involvement of Smith's Electric Vehicles. The business declined and in 1966 Walkers & County Cars was wound up. Prior to this however Eagle had gained the license for the Paladin System and Densmore Walker continued to produce clever and ingenious collecting systems such as his 'Preener system', which featured an in-house packer pressing. When a full bin was ready for collection, a hoist on the vehicle lifted it into position and an in-built scissors system in its base would push the load out!

Of course, many other manufacturers tried their hand with this specialist market, and there are many companies we simply do not know about or have been forgotten by the industry. We hope that this book will stir the recollections of the readers, and we would invite them to write and tell us if they know of any omissions. Meanwhile, the following list of firms who 'dabbled' with refuse vehicles in addition to the more important manufacturers.

AUSTIN CROMPTON PARKINSON ELECTRIC VEHICLES
This company mainly supplied electrical equipment for RCVs.

D. P. BATTERY CO. Grosvenor Gardens, London.

C.R.C.

W & G DU CROSS of Acton

EASYLOADER MOTORS LTD.
Yet another London based company, Easyloader was producing refuse vehicles from 1928, but they were short-lived and wound up in 1931. A new company - New Easyloader Motors Ltd. produced the 'New Easyloader' from 1932 again not lasting very long. The lack of marketing within the company couldn't have helped - they couldn't get away from the term 'easyloader' by the look of it.

F & M MOTORS LTD., of Manor Street Chelsea.

GENERAL VEHICLES
This was another design with American influence that was built at the Farringdon Works, Kings Road, Birmingham. General Vehicles built electric vehicles of 4 and 6 wheel configurations from the 1920s ceasing production around 1935.

GIBSON
Gibson of Edinburgh was another Scottish contender in the refuse collection vehicle market with their 'pendulum' action body.

LEWIN ROAD SWEEPERS
This small manufacturer from West Bromwich used the Oschner system of dustless loading equipment.

LAFFLYS (ENGLAND) CO. LTD., of Kilburn

ALEX LAURIE & SONS
This Falkirk firm produced some semi-trailer bodies for drawing behind both horses and Scammell Mechanical Horse tractors.

Right: *A rare picture of a YEWCO body on a Guy Otter chassis, this system was essentially a Fore & Aft tipper with Spenborough two-way hydraulic tipping gear. The tailgate being equipped with three hydraulic dustless loading bin lifts.* Robin Hannay

Above: *A Lewin-Oschner 'Pakamatic' body on an Albion FT3AL chassis with a 5-man crew cab in Glasgow.* Biggar Museum Trust

NEWEY

VESPA
One delightful yet surprising entrant in this field of minor builders was the Vespa scooter manufacturer who built what had to be one of the must unusual refuse collection vehicles ever. When we say refuse collection vehicles, we mean that in the late 1950s a VESPA scooter complete with side-car collection box could be seen on litter patrol around the streets of St. Helens. Oh for a picture!

YEWCO
The Yorkshire Engineering & Welding Co. was from Idle near Bradford, who imported and assembled the Dutch, De-Graaf, dustless loading system on to UK chassis.

No chaps this is not the end, but the rest of the story is up to you - there's plenty of room for more inside!

ACKNOWLEDGMENTS

In addition to the photographic credits this book could not have been produced with out the kind help and advice from the following people and organisations:

Amberley Museum;
Bill Aldridge;
Frank Bashford;
Bedford Trucks;
Roger F. de Boer;
Andy Ballister;
Biggar Museum, (Albion Archives)
Syd Carroll;
Cargotec (Mark Stapley);

Jim Coombs;
Dennis-Eagle;
Ron Exelby (Londonderry Garage);
Garrett Museum;
S. Grundon & Co;
Ben Heath;
Historic Commercial Vehicle Society;
Robin Hannay;
John Hogarth;
Arthur Ingram;
Institute of Wastes Management;
Derek Jennings;
Brian Lambie;
Lancaster City Corporation;

Rush Green Motors;
Peter Seaword;
Sheffield Corporation;
Shefflex Ltd.;
Suffolk County Council Records Office;
Andy Tett;
Anthony R. Thomas;
Bill Thornycroft;
Dennis Sherer of Vauxhall Motors;
Bob Whewell;
Bob Whitehead;
Jim Wilkinson.
Plus the many others who have helped in one way or another.